Stimulating Creativity and Enquiry

Amy Arnold

Featherstone

Published 2010 by A&C Black Publishers Limited
36 Soho Square, London W1D 3QY
www.acblack.com

ISBN 978-1-4081-2321-8

Text © Amy Arnold 2010
Design Sally Boothroyd 2010

A CIP record for this publication is available from the British Library.

Printed in Great Britain by Latimer Trend & Company Limited

This book is produced using paper that is made from wood grown in
managed, sustainable forests. It is natural, renewable and recyclable.
The logging and manufacturing processes conform to the environmental
regulations of the country of origin.

To see our full range of titles
visit **www.acblack.com**

Contents

Introduction

This book aims to provide practical ideas, support and inspiration on how to stimulate creativity and enquiry in young children through the use of effective questioning.

Our world is full of mystery, wonder and intrigue. Questioning the world around us begins at birth and continues throughout our lifetime. Children naturally and instinctively question situations, events and their own observations long before they have the skills to verbally communicate their thoughts. A cry from a young baby who, using their senses of smell, sound and sight, has realised they don't know the person who is holding them, could well be their means of asking, 'Who are you? Do I know you?' They are expressing their thoughts, making a statement and are beginning to question the growing number of unknowns around them. As a one year old, my own daughter, Evie, had a fabulous appetite – eating ranked high in her list of favourite activities! After eating all of her raisins she held her bowl up, gestured with an upturned hand and verbalised 'gone'. Even without the verbal communication her message would have been understood through her actions and gesture. Her message was refined by repeating the actions, gestures and verbal communication whilst also, adding in a facial expression to add weight to her communications, she was clearly making a statement and asking a question, 'They've all gone, I'm not happy about it. Can I have some more?'

In this way, actions, movement, expression and verbal skills are skilfully and effectively used every day by young children to ask questions – relating to their individual needs and to aid understanding of the world around them.

As development and exploration of the world continues so too does the sophistication of young children's questioning skills. Young children are quite competent at using a range of strategies to ask questions of those around them. Evie, at 18 months old, was in the garden using a hose to fill up a large watering can. She then made several attempts to lift the watering can. Looking puzzled and a little dismayed her facial expressions were asking, 'Why can't I move it? What is happening?' Responding with a question, 'Would you like Mummy to help you?' (whilst bending down), soon met with a determined and independent squeal letting me know 'No!' Just a few minutes later she was still standing by the watering can shouting, 'Mummy?' her method of asking 'Can you help me now?' and letting me know 'Now you can help'.

The importance of a question

Children enter settings and schools with rich, successful and competent questioning skills unique to their own individual characters, it is crucial that these skills are recognised, understood, built upon and extended. Equipping children with the skills, confidence and competence to pose questions will prove to be invaluable in their futures.

Questioning can open the gateway to a whole new world of possibilities, allowing the unknown to be explored, imagined and played with. Questions can promote germination of new, original and creative ideas, offer solutions to problems and give the learner ownership and control of their explorations.

'The important thing is to not stop questioning. Curiosity has its own reason for existing. One cannot help but be in awe when he contemplates the mysteries of eternity; of life; of the marvellous structure of reality...' Einstein, A.

Children's natural inquisitiveness and curiosity about their world can be harnessed by planning and offering irresistible experiences, driven by children's passions and interests. The examples in this book could and should be interpreted in many different ways, depending on individual children, settings, locations and communities.

'Curiosity is the driving force of exploratory play. The desire to know more leads to the development of knowledge, skill and understanding. It is the foundation of a lifetime of experience.' Alison Hutchinson – EYE Volume 10 No 6

Encouraging children to ask questions, wonder and imagine can add a new dimension to experiences and often provide a cognitive shift from the concrete here and now into the abstract unknown. Questioning promotes risk taking, brave explorations and the creation of exciting, fresh and new opportunities. These will be vital skills for our next generation, essential for questioning changes, solving new problems, predicting and planning solutions.

We cannot possibly know what the future may hold, it is uncertain and unknown. We already know that the 21st century is moving at an astonishing pace, particularly in technological advances. We are fortunate to be in the privileged position to be able to inspire and enthuse the next generation to love learning, to question life and grasp the world with passion.

'Each generation will reap what the former generation has sown.' Chinese Proverb

Who is this book for?

This book is for all Early Years professionals and adults working with young children in a range of settings who are seeking a more creative, child-led or personalised approach.

Nursery and Pre-School staff, along with students training for a qualification in working with young children will find this book invaluable. It can be used as a catalyst for stimulating thoughts and ideas into activities which provide young, inquisitive learners the opportunity to question and draw upon their own knowledge. This is essential for children to make sense of the world around them and break through the boundaries of expectation.

Early Years Foundation Stage (EYFS) and Key Stage One (KS1) Teachers, Trainee Teachers and Learning Support Assistants will find this book useful in identifying ways to build upon the questions that children may ask and stimulate further questioning through a range of approaches and activities.

Headteachers, managers and advisers are all aware of the requirement of the EYFS:

'Children are competent learners from birth and develop and learn in a wide variety of ways. All practitioners should, therefore, look carefully at the children in their care, consider their needs, their interests, and their stages of development and use all of this information to help plan a challenging and enjoyable experience across all the areas of Learning and Development.' EYFS Guidance (2008)

This book provides a bridge between the written, detailed requirements and what these requirements look like in practice. It is a clear, hands-on practical resource that can be dipped in and out of and requires very little, if any, financial outlay.

The book is designed to show how the four guiding themes of the EYFS: A Unique Child, Positive Relationships, Enabling Environments and Learning and Development can be encompassed through a range of activities and experiences. As learning experiences and activities are tailored to meet the needs, interests and learning steps of individual children in a range of settings, it is impossible to pre-empt the range of Development Matters Steps and Early Learning Goals that could be encompassed. Examples of the Early Learning Goals which were evident through firsthand experience with individual children are included with some activities to provide a feel and flavour of the direction children's learning could take.

The main aim of the book is to help open up a world of possibilities and begin a journey with the children in your care – from the known into exploring and discovering the unknown.

Inspiring questioning

There are many types of questions which produce different responses and outcomes. Identifying your purpose and reason for questioning should influence the type of question that is asked.

Closed questions usually trigger short responses and are questions where there is normally only one answer. Closed questions give children an opportunity to recall previously acquired information or knowledge.

Closed questions can be used to obtain quick information or set the scene for leading into more open questions. Closed questions are not as cognitively demanding or challenging, but are useful at times, particularly at tidy up time, for example: 'Is the shed open?' 'Where are the musical instruments?' 'Have you turned the hose off?'

Open questions can trigger a wide range of different responses, which are not pre-determined by having to know specific information. They can allow learners to share their unique thoughts and gain an insight into the thoughts and ideas of others. For example: 'Tell me about your rocket?' 'Why do you think the Big Bad Wolf tried to eat Little Red Riding Hood?' 'What do you think it does?'

Open questions can be left wide open: 'What would you have done?' This enables the learner to make their own interpretations of the question and allows teachers and practitioners a greater insight into the thought patterns and perceptions of individual learners. Wide open questions may prove a little challenging for some children and offering a little more detail could help children to focus their thoughts, yet still allow them to voice their ideas, for example: 'What would you have done if you were Little Red Riding Hood / The Wolf / Little Red Riding Hood's Mum?'

Open questions require a greater level of thought; they are more cognitively demanding as there is no right or learned answer. They encourage and invite children to think and generate new ideas, which in turn can inspire further thinking and exploration.

Blooms Taxonomy

In 1956 Benjamin Bloom created a classification system to define and order thinking skills. Bloom's taxonomy identifies six thinking levels, these are ordered according to the intellect and cognitive behaviour required by each level.

Higher Order Thinking Skills

6. Evaluation
Learners develop opinions, make judgements and decisions

5. Synthesis
Learners create or design a new and original idea

4. Analysis
Learners look at chunks of information / learning in detail and then look at how these link together to make the big picture

3. Application
Learners apply prior learning in a new context

2. Comprehension
Learners share their ideas or interpret events in their own words

1. Recall / Knowledge
Learners recall or remember previous learning

Lower Order Thinking Skills

Bloom classified Recall or Knowledge, Comprehension and Application as Lower Order thinking skills and Analysis, Synthesis and Evaluation as Higher order thinking skills.

An example of Blooms taxonomy in action using the story 'Eat your Peas' by Kes Gray and Nick Sharratt

6. Evaluation
Was Daisy successful? Why or Why Not?
Did mum do a good job?

5. Synthesis
What would you have done if you were Daisy?
Could Daisy have eaten her peas? Or pretended too?

4. Analysis
Do you think mum would buy Daisy all of the things?
Which part did you like best?
Did Daisy know all along that mum did not like brussel sprouts?
How do you think Daisy was feeling?

3. Application
What would happen if Daisy did eat her peas?
Would you have eaten the peas?

2. Comprehension
What can you say about Daisy's mum?
Can you tell us about Daisy?

1. Recall / Knowledge
What is Daisy's mum trying to make her eat?
What is Daisy wearing?
What happened in the story?

Blooms taxonomy provides a framework for questioning, essential for planning questions to develop children's higher order thinking skills and consolidate and refine lower order thinking skills. Ultimately, children should become confident and competent in asking and answering questions from all six levels, according to the activity or task they are engaged in.

Understanding and knowing each child well enables practitioners to use questions that are accessible, yet challenging for individual children.

Tips for questioning

1. Sometimes children have intentionally not created something specific, they may have been absorbed in experimenting and exploring without a finished product. A sense of failure could result if they cannot answer, 'What have you made?' or 'What is it?' Using the opener 'Tell me about…' is often more open and less pressured for children to respond to, e.g. 'Wow! Can you tell me about this?' 'Tell me about Goldilocks' breakfast?'

2. Subtle questioning, almost without a question e.g. 'I wonder if… What if we…' then pausing to allow the children to share their thoughts on what the wonder could be or leaving a very open question, e.g. 'I wonder what it would be like to fly?' Again a less pressured way of questioning young children and an encouraging way for children to share their unique thoughts.

3. Giving time to think, imagine and daydream… The most original ideas grow over time and stem from a tiny seed of thought. Children need time to imagine, daydream, explore and build upon their dreams; it could be over a morning, a day, a week, a fortnight or longer.

4. Time to chat! As children question the world around them, giving them time to voice their thoughts and ideas with adults and peers can help to clarify their thinking, enhance and extend their explanations and allow them to refine their ideas, develop language for thinking and aid making connections.

5. Run with their imagination… Wherever possible, fuel their curiosity, plan, resource, test, discuss and evaluate their ideas and value their imaginations. There may be many occasions where there are constraints of space or resources but discussing, working through and designing alternatives provides fantastic learning opportunities.

6. Play Devils' advocate… In a fun and supportive way, challenge children's thinking by responding with possible problems such as, 'Mmm…So how would Spiderman fly?'

7. Take time to re-visit and evaluate, reflecting on the initial questions posed and the investigations that followed – 'What have we discovered / found out?' 'What's the most interesting thing you have found out?' 'Did anything really surprise you?'

8. Sharing answers… Regularly demonstrating and sharing findings and discoveries with large and small groups of children can further motivate and place great importance on their investigations, as well as developing confidence and communication skills.

9. Pass everyday problems over to children – 'How do we know how many snacks we will need?' 'How can we share six oranges between us?' 'How will we know if someone has watered the peas?'

10. Watch and listen as children are busy playing and learning and, if appropriate, sensitively intervene with questions to support and challenge. 'Is there anything that could help you carry the heavy bucket to the digging zone?'

11. Grasp spontaneity… Value and fuel children's spontaneous questions and thoughts, the ideas which seem to come from nowhere and have no connections to previous or current events or experiences.

How does inspiring questioning relate to the EYFS curriculum?

Questioning flows throughout all areas of learning and often connects and intertwines learning areas together, both questions which children pose and questions which adults use to challenge and extend, during child-initiated and adult led or directed activities.

As questions open up a whole new world of possibilities children will explore, plan, create, share, predict and, with careful questioning, evaluate and refine.

As children explore and investigate, following their unique thoughts and interests, it provides a base for building communication, problem solving, decision making, creative, critical and sustained thinking.

Questioning can support effective implementation of **all areas of learning and development** as recommended by EYFS Guidance:

Creative Development
'Children's creativity must be extended by the provision of support for their curiosity, exploration and play. They must be provided with opportunities to explore and share their thoughts, ideas and feelings.' EYFS Statutory Framework 2007

Physical Development
'They must be supported in using all of their senses to learn about the world around them and to make connections between new information and what they already know.' EYFS Statutory Framework 2007

Knowledge and Understanding of the World
'Children must be supported in developing the knowledge, skills and understanding that help them to make sense of the world. Their learning must be supported through offering opportunities for them to use a range of tools safely; encounter creatures, people, plants and objects in their natural environments and in real-life situations; undertake practical 'experiments'; and work with a range of materials.' EYFS Statutory Framework 2007

Problem Solving, Reasoning and Numeracy
'Children must be supported in developing their understanding of Problem Solving, Reasoning and Numeracy in a broad range of contexts in which they can explore, enjoy, learn, practise and talk about their developing understanding.' EYFS Statutory Framework 2007

Communication, Language and Literacy
'Children's learning and competence in communicating, speaking and listening, being read to and beginning to read and write must be supported and extended. They must be provided with opportunity and encouragement to use their skills in a range of situations and for a range of purposes, and be supported in developing the confidence and disposition to do so.' EYFS Statutory Framework 2007

Personal, Social and Emotional Development
'Children must be provided with experiences and support which will help them to develop a positive sense of themselves and of others; respect for others; social skills; and a positive disposition to learn. Providers must ensure support for children's emotional well-being to help them to know themselves and what they can do.' EYFS Statutory Framework 2007

Throughout this book many examples and activities have Early Learning Goals linked to them. When children are actively involved in questioning, imagining, wondering and sharing their findings, the following Early Learning Goals are naturally developing:

Personal, Social and Emotional Development

- Continue to be interested, excited and motivated to learn
- Be confident to try new activities and speak in a familiar group
- Maintain attention, concentration and sit quietly when appropriate
- Respond to significant experiences, showing a range of feelings when appropriate
- Form good relationships with adults and peers
- Work as part of a group or class, taking turns and sharing fairly
- Select and use activities and resources independently

Communication, Language and Literacy

- Interact with others, negotiating plans and activities and taking turns in conversation
- Enjoy listening to and using spoken and written language, and readily turn to it in their play and learning
- Sustain attentive listening, responding to what they have heard with relevant comments, questions or actions
- Extend their vocabulary exploring the meanings and sounds of new words
- Speak clearly and audibly with confidence and control showing awareness of the listener
- Use language to imagine and recreate roles and experiences
- Use talk to organise, sequence and clarify thinking, ideas, feelings and events

Problem Solving, Reasoning and Numeracy

- Use developing mathematical ideas and methods to solve practical problems
- Describe solutions to practical problems, drawing on experience, talking about ideas, methods and choices. (Development matters)

Knowledge and Understanding of the World

- Investigate objects and materials by using all of their senses as appropriate
- Ask questions about why things happen and how things work
- Observe, find out about and identify features in the place they live and the natural world

Creative Development

- Respond in a variety of ways to what they see, hear, smell, touch and feel
- Express and communicate their ideas, thoughts and feelings by using a widening range of materials, suitable tools, imaginative and role-play, movement, designing and making, and a variety of songs and musical instruments
- Use their imagination in art and design, music, dance, imaginative and role-play and stories

How does inspiring questioning relate to the KS1 curriculum?

Hands on, purposeful and meaningful learning is as crucial in Key Stage One (and all phases of education) as in the Early Years Foundation Stage. Appealing and exciting experiences engage and stimulate learners to question and explore, seeking out their own preferred path of investigation based on their interests and motivations.

Inspiring children to wonder and question and providing challenge through planned questioning, alongside practical activities, is perfect for building on children's Early Years Foundation Stage experience and skills in Key Stage One.

Effective questioning can support the National Curriculum aim:

'By providing rich and varied contexts for pupils to acquire, develop and apply a broad range of knowledge, understanding and skills, the curriculum should enable pupils to think creatively and critically, to solve problems and to make a difference for the better. It should give them the opportunity to become creative, innovative, enterprising and capable of leadership to equip them for their future lives as workers and citizens.'
National Curriculum

Questions which arise from everyday, real situations can support the values and purpose of the National Curriculum, as below:

'Education must enable us to respond positively to the opportunities and challenges of the rapidly changing world in which we live and work'.
National Curriculum – Values and Purpose

*'Tell me, I'll forget,
Show me, I'll remember,
Let me do it, I'll understand.'*
Chinese Proverb

The activities and ideas presented in this book can easily be adapted and lend themselves towards development of the following areas of Key Stage One Programme of Study:

Literacy
- Speaking
- Listening and Responding
- Group Discussion and Interaction
- Drama

Numeracy
- Using and applying mathematics

Science
- Scientific Enquiry

ICT
- Finding things out
- Developing ideas and making things happen
- Exchanging and sharing information
- Reviewing, modifying and evaluating work as it progresses

History
- Historical Enquiry
- Organisation and Communication

Design and Technology
- Developing, planning and communicating ideas
- Evaluating processes and products

Geography
- Geographical and enquiry skills

Art and Design
- Exploring and developing ideas
- Evaluating and developing work

Music
- Responding and reviewing (appraising and listening skills)

P.E.
- Evaluating and improving performance

PSHE
- Developing confidence and responsibility and making the most of their abilities
- Developing good relationships and respecting differences

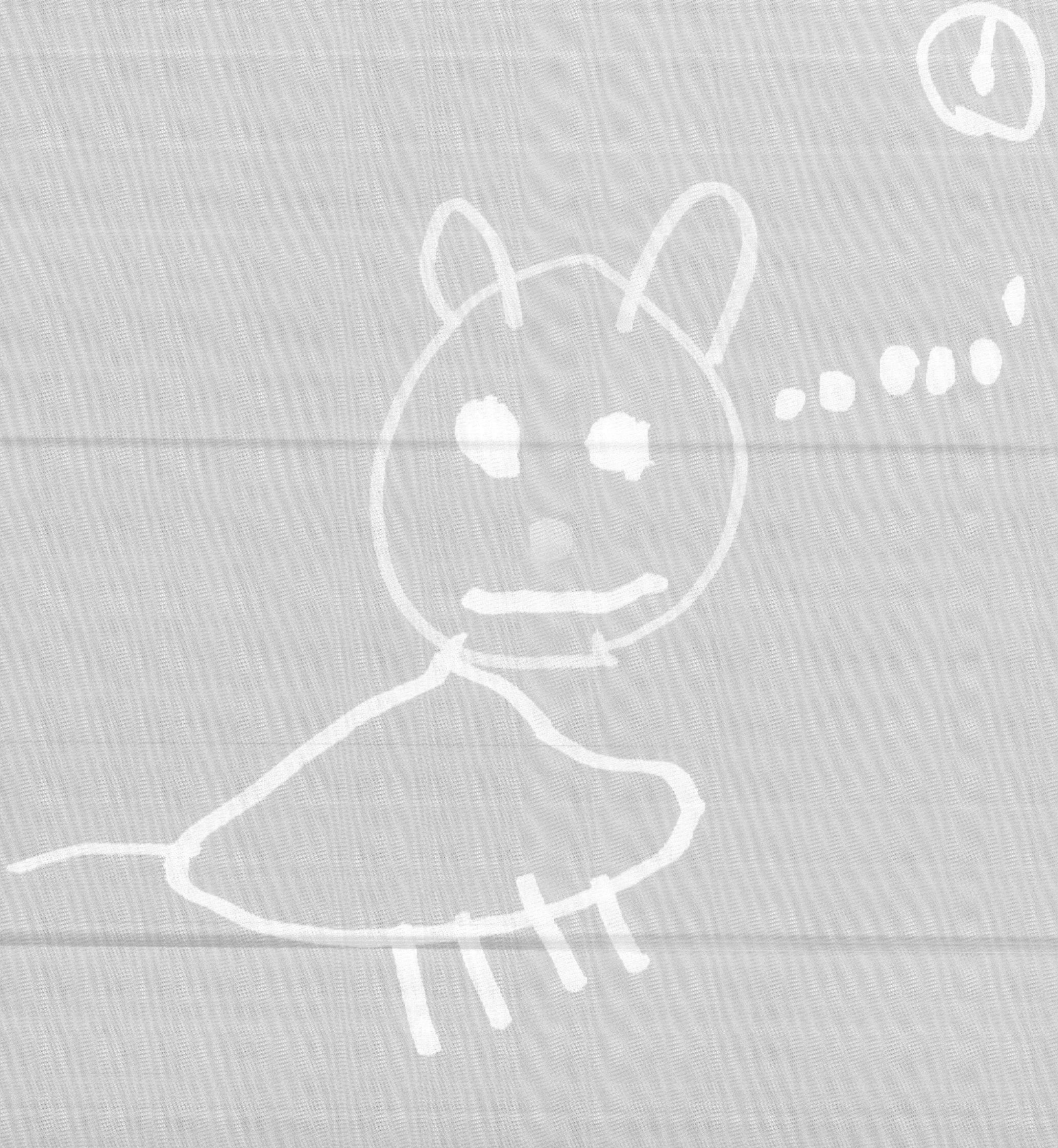

Wondering, Daydreaming and Imagining –
child-led learning adventures

Wondering, Daydreaming and Imagining

'Imagination is more important than knowledge.'
Einstein, A

As adults, our most creative thoughts can often be at a time when our mind is wandering, imagining and going beyond the known here and now, and venturing into new areas and making links which have previously appeared to have no connections.

Allowing the mind to wander can often infuse humour, relaxation, creativity, answers to questions or solutions to problems.

The language of questioning is a powerful tool for going beyond the known and into a world of dreams and endless possibilities.

Young children have often developed a great sense of humour, this can be a powerful motivator in enabling children to make links, imagine and sustain thinking.

Creative pupils are curious, question and challenge, and don't always follow rules.

They:

♦ ask 'why?' 'how?' 'what if?'

♦ ask unusual questions

♦ respond to ideas, questions, tasks or problems in a surprising way

♦ challenge conventions and their own and others' assumptions

♦ think independently.   National Curriculum 2008

What if…?

What if questions fit seamlessly into all aspects of the day: during a story, getting ready to go home, when exploring or role playing, mark making or painting – there are no boundaries.

During a shared story, pause and ponder on a given page and think aloud… 'I'm just wondering… What If… (The children may well offer their own suggestions here – go with them!) …the tooth fairy did not have any wings?'

Ensure that the children have time to process and think the question through, as well as share their thoughts with a partner or the people around them. It is great for practitioners to be at eye level with the children – listening and responding to children's ideas or noting their unique thoughts.

Invite children to share their ideas with the group, celebrate the wide range of ideas. 'Wow! Daniel thinks that the tooth fairy would need a skateboard and Abigail thinks that she would be able to magic herself some wings. What amazing ideas!'

Asking what if questions could be a simple discussion in pairs, small or large groups or it could be the beginning of several weeks of investigating and exploring: Can we test out the skateboard? Could we make a bag for the tooth fairy?

Make links with home by encouraging children, 'Don't forget to ask Mummy or Grandad "What if the tooth fairy didn't have wings?"'

Write on a board outside or pin a quick notice up in your setting's collection area to let parents and carers know what the children have been thinking about that day. It is often intriguing the ideas that grown-ups come back with; just like the children, they are often linked to their firsthand experiences, areas of work or interests.

Look for what ifs everywhere:

What if… The caterpillar wasn't hungry?

What if… Kyle's baby sister could talk?

What if… The sea was made of sand and the sand was made of sea? (a week long topic on boats and floating and sinking followed this question!)

What if… Mermaids came to visit our school / nursery / class?

What if… The sky was made of grass?

What if… Cows made strawberry milkshakes?

'In 1995 Howard Gardener expanded his original list of seven intelligences by adding an eighth; the naturalist intelligence.'
Campbell & Dickinson 1994

Children are naturally curious and constantly questioning the world around them. Developing children's confidence to share their thoughts and ideas with their friends and key familiar adults, can lead to a greater understanding of each child's unique curiosities, interests and needs.

'The opportunity to follow personal curiosity allows incidental discoveries, often completely different from what may have been pre-planned; outcomes are often at a more complex level than would have been anticipated. Everyone succeeds; there is no right or wrong way, no correct answer or end product.'
Alison Hutchison – EYE Volume 10 No 6

I wonder…

Model, demonstrate and actively engage children in wondering. Using the question opener I wonder… can lead to a far more personalised learning journey, bespoke to children's individual thoughts.

The following example shows how one child's I wonder… (about a whale) ignited a spark in many children, particularly those with a real passion for the natural world.

I wonder… Why whales are so big? This initial question posed by Poppy, a 4-year-old girl, led to a sea creature rescue centre being set up outside, which inspired and engaged a group of children for almost a week!

The learning cycle of questioning, predicting, researching, testing and evaluating took off at a rapid pace. Collaboratively resources were gathered and tasks identified 'We need to weigh them to see how big they are!' After lots of hands-on exploration, decision making, estimating and checking predictions using different sea creatures, the evaluation showed that, 'We still don't know if the whale is the biggest!'

The cycle began again, as children compared the length of the whale against other sea creatures. Adults supported and challenged the children with questions and statements, such as, 'Oh I see, so the biggest sea creature is the longest one?'

As learners discovered that Octopi use ink to scare away any predators and have suction rings on their tentacles, this caused many further questions. Memorable questions included: 'If you cut an octopus open would the ink all come out?' 'I have suckers on my car window toy, are they like that?' A trip to the local fishmongers provided the resources necessary to observe, investigate, research and hopefully draw conclusions to the questions raised.

Providing children with meaningful, firsthand experiences can promote deep, true and lifelong learning.

'It is their desire and determination to do real things, not in the future, but right now, that gives children the curiosity, energy, determination and patience to learn all they learn.' Holt, J.

Children communicated their findings so far, 'No, the starfish was really heavy but only has short legs'. As an investigation into measuring length took place the opportunity for observing and understanding where children were currently at with their PSRN development was invaluable.

Exploration and investigation through the sea creature rescue centre continued for almost a week, other children dipped in and out, but a highly absorbed group of four children remained there at all times! On day three the children decided that 'because they are only toys, we don't know if it's true', with a sensitive practitioner prompting and questioning, 'Mmm, what we could do?' 'Oh so we need to find out about real sea creatures, how could we do that?' This led seamlessly into carrying out research using information books, the internet and writing letters to a sea life centre.

Children were intrigued and fascinated to closely examine real sea creatures; the aroma caused many discussions and a great opportunity for extending vocabulary!

A daily news update by Sea-life Rescue Staff, provided at the end of each session, always invited 'Come and look at the posters, or see the animals in their enclosure'.

An initial 'I wonder' question provided the framework for linking all areas of learning and these Early Learning Goals:

◆ Use developing mathematical ideas and methods to solve practical problems

◆ Use language such as 'greater', 'smaller', 'heavier' or 'lighter' to compare quantities

◆ Investigate objects and materials by using all of their senses as appropriate

◆ Find out about, and identify, some features of living things, objects and events they observe

◆ Look closely at similarities, differences, patterns and change

◆ Ask questions about why things happen and how things work

◆ Use information and communication technology to support their learning

◆ Continue to be interested, excited and motivated to learn

◆ Be confident to try new activities, initiate ideas and speak in a familiar group

◆ Work as part of a group or class, taking turns and sharing fairly

◆ Select and use activities and resources independently

◆ Interact with others, negotiating plans and activities and taking turns in conversation

◆ Enjoy listening to and using spoken and written language and readily turn to it in their play and learning

◆ Use language to imagine and recreate roles and experiences

◆ Use talk to organise, sequence and clarify thinking, ideas, feelings and events

◆ Show an understanding of how information can be found in non-fiction texts to answer questions about where, who, why and how

◆ Attempt writing for different purposes

So easily, could the question 'I wonder… Why whales are so big?' have covered a wide range of Literacy and Numeracy Objectives, as well as, many aspects of the National Curriculum Programme of study across all subjects for both Key Stage One and Key Stage Two and beyond.

Which raises the interesting question, should learners' questions and thoughts influence the themes and topics across all phases of education?

It's a set up!

The learning environment is crucial in ensuring that children feel safe and secure, whilst also stimulating children's thoughts and questions, leading to rich learning opportunities.

Enabling Environments is one of the four themes of the EYFS and the principle clearly communicates:

'The environment plays a key role in supporting and extending children's development and learning.' EYFS 2008

By occasionally bringing a new and unknown, yet safe and stimulating change to both the indoor and outdoor learning environment, a world of possibilities opens up and lends itself well to children developing their own direction and path of discovery.

The EYFS Guidance urges us to *'Create an indoor environment that is reassuring and comforting for all children, while providing interest through novelty from time to time.'*

The following pages show how setting up a few simple resources and props could bring a new, fresh and exciting sense of discovery to both indoor and outdoor learning environments. As learners follow their own paths of interest and enquiry, the examples show how the four themes of the EYFS are supported and intertwined.

Paws for thought

The stimulus

One simple way to spark children's imagination and give opportunity for children to draw upon their previous experiences is to arrange a trail of paw prints across the ceiling, ready for the children to discover the next day!

Ignite children's enthusiasm and excitement by gasping and showing expressions of shock and surprise, alongside them.

Provide countless opportunities for children to follow their own ideas by offering sentence starters such as, I wonder… What if… Maybe… What? Why? How? allowing children time to think and share their ideas as they develop.

Talk it through

Support children with processing their thoughts as together you tackle the important questions:

I wonder…

Who – *they belong to?*

What – *did they look like?*

How – *did they get here / up there?*

Why – *have they come here?*

When – *did they visit?*

Who – *saw them?*

Where – *are they now?*

Investigate and Explore

Encourage children to share their suggestions and pose their own questions. Follow up on the initial stimulus of the paw prints across the ceiling by equipping areas of the learning environment with resources to further support and test children's ideas and suggestions as they emerge.

Outdoor area
Large netting
A jar of honey hidden outside!
Binoculars
Safari hats
Rucksacks
Magnifying glasses
Large chalks and brushes

Writing area
Paw shaped paper
Clipboards and paper with a paw logo on them
Notebooks
Mini books – shaped as a bear head
Paw print pencils / stamps
Equipment for children to make their own books – stapler, paper, scissors, sellotape

Book area
Selection of bear stories including the classics: *We're going on a bear hunt, Goldilocks and the Three Bears* and *Brown Bear, Brown Bear What do you see?*

Arts and Crafts area
Selection of fabrics and material
Paper in assorted shapes and sizes
Mark making materials
Paints

Children will be enabled to design, create, imagine and communicate their ideas whilst following their chosen path of enquiry by having the freedom to access and transport resources from all areas of the setting.

These are just a few ideas – as children's thoughts and ideas develop the learning environment could look very different, maybe following a monster theme, a lion theme or even the chilly north pole should a polar bear be discovered!

A Unique Child	Support for each child's individual ideas and thoughts, which could have stemmed from a favourite story, a trip to the zoo, a chat with granddad, a television programme, a holiday. Valuing and respecting each child as a unique individual. Providing opportunity for children to further their ideas through careful resourcing and supporting of their original thoughts.
Positive Relationships	Supporting children to become independent and confident in sharing their ideas and developing strong relations with their peers as they listen to one another's thoughts and ideas. Developing children's confidence in identifying, collecting and transporting resources around the setting.
Enabling Environments	Subtly starting with a trail of paw prints across the ceiling and developing out into all areas of the environment dependent on children's interests, ideas and chosen path of enquiry. An environment where children can access a wide range of resources to support their investigating, creating and discovering.
Learning and Development	◆ Collaborating and sharing ideas and thoughts ◆ Talk for a variety of purposes ◆ Listening to the ideas of others and contributing to others' ideas ◆ Imagining and wondering ◆ Asking questions / answering questions

Open for interpretation

The stimulus

Bunting can be created cheaply using paper triangles and ribbon or string. The colour of the bunting *could* play a big part in children's interpretation and direction of play and learning. Attaching brightly coloured red, blue, green and yellow bunting to an area of the setting can be the catalyst to a wide range of play activities, initiated by children's interpretation of the bunting. Following children's thoughts with open and sensitive questions can lead to a personalised, unique and child-led learning adventure.

Talk it through

As children discover the bunting across the carpet area of the room, the most amazing discussions could emerge. This opportunity for assessment through observation may demonstrate each child's skills in communicating both verbally and using gestures, as well as their skills in listening, interpreting, reasoning, predicting and summarising.

Allowing children adequate time to share their excitement and ideas can instil deeper ownership of learning opportunities and activities that naturally follow. Helping children to 'scaffold' and build upon their thoughts requires sensitive support and questioning such as:

That sounds interesting... Tell me about it?

Wow! A Circus! Can you tell me about the circus?

I love your idea... What would happen next? What would you need?

A party! Simon was talking about a party, can you share your ideas with him?

It's a castle? That sounds really exciting!

Support children's thoughts and ideas through enabling them to identify how they could, and what they would need to follow, their chosen learning path.

How could we make a big top?

What would your knight like to do in his castle?

What would we need for a party?

Investigate and Explore

Taking the question 'How could we make a big top?', for example, can easily lead a group of eager learners to begin constructing a big top; this could be supported throughout the learning environment by providing resources and activities to complement the initial and emerging ideas.

Outdoor area
Large boxes
Colourful large fabric pieces
Large frame / Climbing frame
Paints
Large pieces of paper – essential for creating signs!
Balls
Hoops
Skipping ropes
Balancing beams / chalk lines / ropes
Stilts

Writing area

> Mirroring the theme in the writing area with 'mini' bunting, colourful fabric, pictures and words or posters relating to the children's identified theme can create an irresistible urge for children to explore the area.

Brightly coloured shaped paper
Paper with a circus logo
Examples of and equipment to make tickets, posters, leaflets and invitations

Book area

Display of books relating to themes and interests identified by children:

The Kiss that missed, Good Night Sleep Tight, The Three Wishes (All by David Melling), *Spot goes to the circus* (by Eric Hill), *Into the Castle* (Usborne picture books)
Harlequin patterned fabric / cushions / beanbags
Leaflets from the circus, local castles
Circus-linked masks – clowns, ringmaster, animals

Arts and Crafts area

Lollipop sticks
Sellotape, masking tape, glue
Coloured paper or fabric pieces (for creating their own big top)
Dowel wood, hammers, nails
String or ribbon (for maybe making bunting)

Small World Play

Sand and glitter base, toy animals, finger puppets, lollipop stick puppets, small hoops (curtain rings)

Messy Play area

Equipment and ingredients for making jelly or custard!

These ideas are focused towards a circus or possible castle theme. The environment may look very different if learners are fizzing with excitement relating to a party theme!

Alternatively, the colour of the bunting may influence children's ideas. I have seen a group of girls inspired by pink and purple bunting leading to them spending a week immersing themselves in all areas linked to princesses and castles.

What ideas could stem from black and white bunting?

A Unique Child	Children are an integral part of identifying and creating the learning context and enjoy interacting with others. Children can choose their preferred method of communicating and learning through a wide choice of learning activities and opportunities.
Positive Relationships	Practitioners observe children with sensitivity and encourage creativity and learning by using these observations to build upon children's interests and understanding.
Enabling Environments	Children are supported by the resources and activities set up to inspire them to investigate further and follow their own lines of enquiry. Children have free access to move and transport resources across all areas of the environment, for example: taking books from the reading area outside or using a writing toolkit in the construction area.
Learning and Development	◆ Making links with prior experiences ◆ Talk for a variety of purposes ◆ Making and telling stories ◆ Gross Motor Skill Development ◆ Asking questions / answering questions

Spellbinding

The stimulus

A simple addition to the outdoor learning environment can provide an opportunity for children to question, imagine, explore, make links, investigate and summarise:

Children arrive to discover a witch's broomstick sticking out of the ground and a witch's hat hanging on the fence!

Talk it through

Embrace and expand on children's natural inquisitiveness by listening to their ideas relating to the discovery of the items outside. Encourage children to listen to the ideas and opinions of their friends. Support them to deepen and extend their thoughts by asking open questions such as:

Wow! What a great idea – can you tell me more about it?

I wonder when that happened?

Did you hear Cameron's idea – could you share your ideas together?

Oh so you think that…

As ideas begin to emerge and develop, scribing a list together with groups of children provides a fabulous opportunity for shared writing and capturing children's thoughts and ideas as they develop, as well as eliciting any further questions that may arise.

Investigate and Explore

The possibilities are endless, as are the original, creative and priceless ideas offered by young inspired learners.

Children's learning adventures could take any direction, for example:

◆ A witch may have been searching for treasure – leading to a treasure hunt theme!

◆ It was left from a fancy dress party – leading to a party/costume adventure

◆ It could be linked to a familiar story, (such as, *Room on the Broom* by Julia Donaldson and Alex Sheffler) with children creating or re-telling their own stories.

Investigative area
Spooky shapes or sequins set in orange / blackcurrant jelly for children to carefully remove using tweezers, small spoons or other implements

Ingredients for mixing and making black playdough

Pumpkins, magnifying glasses, trays for seeds, spoons for hollowing, carving tools

Arts and Crafts area
Small twigs and sticks, raffia or twine for making mini broomsticks

Paper and card for making witches hats

Templates for making hanging bats or cats

Book area
A collection of themed books including *Meg & Mog*; *Room on the Broom*; *Funnybones*; Non-fiction books on cats

---

Familiar stories are like a favourite snuggle blanket for children (and adults!) they can provide a safe and secure background to exploring ideas and activities that stem from the text.

Using Meg and Mog as the familiar story, which children investigate further, could see a spooky but friendly learning environment.

Writing area

Add a sparkle of magic to the writing area by enclosing the area with either a canopy of fabric or hanging tissue paper strips in spooky colours of black, white and orange. Use a cauldron shaped container (often used for planting flowers) to store paper or writing implements in.

Spell templates
Coloured paper – black, orange, dark blue
Shaped paper – cauldron, witches hat, pumpkin
Chalk to experiment writing on black paper
Mini books for children to create their own stories

Outdoor area

Create a den for Meg – using fabric or camouflage netting

Make a potion station with bottles and mixing materials including bowls, spoons, whisks and tea strainers ensure children have access to materials to create and bottle their own potions e.g. leaves, sticks, petals.

Writing toolkit for creating labels for bottles or ingredients list.

A Unique Child	Using a familiar and 'comfortable' story each child has the opportunity to hook into and investigate an area they feel comfortable with. It could be exploring, playing at cats or making potions.
Positive Relationships	Practitioners share important information on a daily basis with parents and carers. Parents and carers come into the setting in the morning, sharing what they have seen outside and ideas about where it may have come from.
Enabling Environments	A potentially 'spooky' topic can be explored in a safe, supportive environment that allows children to play and experiment with activities and feel comfortable.
Learning and Development	<ul><li>Investigating objects and materials</li><li>Handling a variety of tools and construction items</li><li>Sharing thoughts and ideas with others</li><li>Mark making</li><li>Reading and maybe re-telling</li></ul>

Control Panel

The stimulus

Imaginative use of a large piece of cardboard, from a redundant box, could be the catalyst for the most original and extended stories:

Measure and cut a piece large piece of cardboard to fit a particular area and cover with silver paint, shiny paper or fabric. Attach on bottle tops and small pieces of sponge (control buttons) and a display screen for writing on (white laminated paper?) and maybe a viewing panel.

Leave plenty of room for children to add lots more buttons, dials and switches.

Attach the large control panel to the allocated space.

Talk it through

As the children discover the 'unfinished' control panel observe and note their reactions and the questions which they raise.

Gather as a group and share the captured children's questions, following their direction of answering the questions and determining the direction of play and learning.

An example of children's questions:

What is it?

Who put it there?

Is it from Doctor Who?

Did the spaceman put it there?

Does it work?

Will it light up?

Follow the children's direction and respond with resources and opportunities to allow them to test, play with, apply and build on their ideas.

It could easily become an aeroplane, submarine, rocket, train or anything that young enquiring minds may imagine!

As ideas begin to flow, instil excitement and facilitate children's cognitive development by asking questions, which lead to creating an environment and climate for playing and learning for extended periods of time:

Wow! You think it's from a spaceship – Tell me all about your idea.

That sounds fascinating!

Can you think of a way we could make a spaceship?

What might you need?

Oh so am I right in thinking you need big boxes with a door and some shiny fabric?

And buttons! Wow! I wonder what the buttons could be used for?

Practitioners can support children's development, across all areas of learning, from the ideas identified by learners in responseto the mystery control panel.

Investigate and Explore

Arts and Crafts area

Empty bottles, shiny paper, card and felt tips for making rockets and their occupants

Variety of materials and fabric, pipe cleaners, googly eyes for making inhabitants from different planets

Large scale boxes and fabric for creating indoor and outdoor spaceships, rockets, launching pads and space centres

Writing area

Paper with letter head from the control panel

Timetables of space launches

Shaped paper for making signs and labels for rockets and spaceships

Paper with an illustrated alien theme – useful for invitations, notes and letters.

Themed area with silver or foil covered tables and chairs.

Number and Problem Solving

Incorporated through all areas with questions such as:

How could you fit 6 astronauts in the spaceship?

When will we know it's time to blast off?

Message from control centre: The rocket is too heavy to take off.

5 little men in a flying saucer – rhyme and props.

How to catch a star by Oliver Jeffers

Star making activities using lollipop sticks, playdough, and paint

---

Book area

A range of fiction and non-fiction space or alien linked texts
For example: *Aliens love underpants* by Claire Freedman, *Here come the Aliens* by Colin McNaughton, *Roaring Rockets* by Tony Mitton, *Q Pootle 5* by Nick Butterworth, *Sun, Moon and Stars* by Usborne Books.

A Unique Child	Developing children's confidence in thinking and following through their original ideas, creating a shared and exciting platform for playing and learning.
Positive Relationships	Showing and sharing excitement and intrigue with children's individual and shared ideas. Listening carefully to children's ideas unfolding and giving prompts to challenge and develop learning.
Enabling Environments	Beginning with children's initial ideas, planning and equipping all areas of the learning environment to inspire children to find out more and further explore. Distilling children's abundance of ideas into manageable focus areas e.g. Space, The Moon, Aliens.
Learning and Development	◆ Imagining and role-playing ◆ Problem Solving ◆ Exploring shape and space in 3D ◆ Sharing thoughts and ideas with others ◆ Sustaining shared thinking

Take a seat

The stimulus

Everyday items arranged in a different way could generate new ideas; leading to a new world of discovery, largely based on children's firsthand experiences.

Creating an arrangement of chairs similar to the layout below can be very enticing!

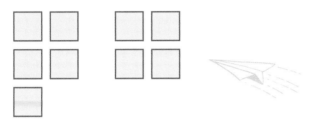

Experimenting with different layouts of equipment, in different areas of the setting, proves fascinating as children apply their knowledge and understanding based on previous firsthand experiences. It also gives children the message that chairs and furniture can be moved to accommodate their play and ideas.

Placing a single chair at the front, for many groups of learners, creates a feeling of someone being in charge or control.

Talk it through

Setting up the above layout of chairs has seen a myriad of different discussions and role-play contexts including travelling in an aeroplane, bus or train, being a teacher with a class of children, a stage with the single chair used for performers' hats and props, a talk by a zookeeper (using animal puppets) and an author signing books!

Observing children as they share their thoughts and ideas can be invaluable for identifying the wide range of children's collective prior experiences and developing an understanding of children's personalities.

Is there a dominant character that instantly creates an aeroplane? A persuasive character who promises dancing and singing for her audience? Or a resourceful child who rushes off to make tickets and bring in animal puppets for the zoo show?

This type of set up provides opportunities for key workers to get to know their children even better, through sharing past experiences and events.

The set up of chairs is the very beginning in resourcing, through skilful questioning of ideas further resources can be included from the children's starting points.

Here we look at how the aeroplane idea can spiral across the setting.

Investigate and Explore

Outdoor area
Flags, chalks, marker cones, goggles, gloves for guiding in aeroplanes

Crates, walkie-talkies, clipboards, large scale construction, maps, aeroplane information books, binoculars for a control tower

Role-play area
Ticket office – badges, hats, paper, clipboards, hole-punch, telephone and writing implements (for checking passengers in).

Aeroplane – passengers, flight attendants, kitchen area at the back of chairs, trays, teacups, food (for serving passengers), and magazines.

Writing Area / Toolkits

Travel linked writing implements (e.g. aeroplane pencils), model aeroplanes and airport posters.

Paper, card, booklets and stampers – to make tickets, menus and passports for passengers.

Selection of fabric and materials to make tactile books

Construction / Arts and Crafts area

Making aircrafts – creating aircraft, hangers, control towers, homes for the workers

Constructing airport shops and restaurants

Book area

Display texture books made by children, inspired by *That's not my plane* by Fiona Watt and Rachel Wells

Tickets, posters and leaflets from airports or travel agents

Fiction and Non fiction books based on countries, airports, planes and flying

Book collection may include: Early atlases, *Going on a plane* (Usborne first experiences), *A day at the airport* by Richard Scarry, *Jeremy* (Thomas and Friends), *Touch and Feel Planes* by Edward Eaves.

A Unique Child	Embracing the diversity of children's prior experiences and using this to influence learning across the setting.
Positive Relationships	Working towards children understanding feelings and interacting positively to ensure all children have the opportunity to discuss and allow their ideas to be heard and explored.
Enabling Environments	Starting with children's firsthand experiences and planning activities to stimulate and extend previous learning and introduce new skills.
Learning and Development	◆ Collaborative learning ◆ Initiating ideas ◆ Connecting to prior experiences ◆ Using imagination ◆ Extending vocabulary

Exploring Explorers

The stimulus

Leaving a trail of clues can build an air of mystery – creating suspense, predictions and a bubbling excitement!

The trail begins with clue one: a pair of binoculars is left in the carpet area where the children gather, along with an envelope with a little detective style magnifying glass logo in the corner. Inside the card reads: *'Under a log you will find where I am going'.*

Talk it through

Practitioners read aloud the clue, children begin to ask questions to find out more information and make sense of the clue:

Is it the log over there? (pointing to dinosaur small world)

Or the one in the outdoor area? (Gives the subliminal message that everyday natural items can be used effectively indoors in different contexts.)

Look a clue! (pointing to the magnifying glass logo) *He needs our help?*

Does he want us to find him?

It may be a lady. How do you know it's a man?

Who is it?

Summarise the children's thoughts and questions and give control over to them, to determine how the investigation will unfold:

Ah! So the problems are… we don't know which log it is or if it is a man or a lady writing to us?

Can we find a way to answer these questions?

As eager learners rush around the setting (not all, some are far too busy being princesses and building zoos!) they are actively engaged in making predictions, planning and recalling the information from the first clue.

Clue two is discovered outside by the logs, along with a map. The trail and questioning pattern continues with practitioners summing up the children's ideas and questions and supporting them in planning the next steps.

When all of the clues and items have been discovered children group together to reflect on the items: binoculars, map, clipboard, rucksack, a large coiled rope. The last clue is:

Thank you for helping me to find all the things. Can you think what I use them for? Who do you think I am?

Observe and note children making links with stories, experiences from the past or recalling scenes from television programmes or computer games – value children's proficiency in today's multimedia world. Practitioners could share with children if they have seen the equipment used before.

Following the pattern of responding to the ideas and stories created by the children, be on hand to offer prompts to promote **higher order thinking** and guide children towards possible resources which could enhance role-play or investigations.

As Rapunzel is rescued, baddies are trapped and the safari is underway, observe and note the skills, language and thought processes that are evident.

A Unique Child	As the coiled rope is tested to its full potential children discover the boundaries of role play and develop understanding of keeping everyone safe.
Positive Relationships	Children develop confidence under the watchful eye of a key person guiding and supporting children to communicate their ideas and find ways to test them out.
Enabling Environments	Starting with children's firsthand experiences and planning activities to stimulate and extend previous learning and introduce new skills.
Learning and Development	◆ Personalising learning ◆ Problem solving ◆ Responding to what they see, hear, think and feel ◆ Recreating experiences and roles ◆ Decision making

Magic and Mystery in Everyday Items –

adult-led learning adventures

Magic and Mystery in Everyday Items –
adult-led learning adventures

Materials and items that we take for granted everyday provide a real source of fascination for children if they are allowed to freely explore and experiment all the possibilities they have to offer.

Involve children and families in collecting materials and objects – amazing collections can soon be built up with very little financial outlay.

Allowing children freedom in independently accessing and transporting resources across and around their learning environments (indoor and outdoor) can greatly enhance play and support their chosen path of investigating and creating. This freedom helps to create the best conditions for development across all areas of learning and setting imaginations and dreams free.

All of the following items and objects can be placed in baskets around the learning environment, ready for children to access and explore.

Ensure that children have ample time to independently explore and test the objects before challenging and questioning children. Observations could show children asking their own questions and discovering their own answers such as: What is it? What can it do? How does it work? What can I do with it?

Careful observation will provide practitioners with an understanding of children's discoveries and allow them to sensitively challenge children to follow their own path of discovery.

Seeing seeds

Health and Safety Alert

This activity may not be suitable for very young children. Remember to check for any children that may have a nut allergy before bringing seeds and nuts into the learning environment.

Always supervise an activity with very small pieces.

Remember to check that no seeds are poisonous to touch or if ingested.

'Natural materials have very high play value and contribute to all major areas of development. As resources for play they are entirely open-ended and can be used in a myriad of different ways.' Jan White – Playing and Learning Outdoors

A collection of seeds in contrasting sizes such as very small poppy seeds to large stones or husks such as an avocado stone or coconut could lead to rich learning opportunities from exploring textures and ordering sizes to imagining what may grow!

Resources

- A wide and varied collection of seeds, for example poppy, sunflower, runner bean, pea, pumpkin, dandelion, conker, avocado and coconut.

- A selection of different sized containers from tiny lids to small pots up to empty ice cream tubs

- Tweezers, small scoops, teaspoons and tablespoons

- Magnifying glasses, notebooks and writing implements

- Standard and non standard equipment for measuring or weighing

- Pots and soil for planting seeds

- Camera

- Pestle and mortar

Questions to consider

After children have had the opportunity to initiate their own play and discovery of the seeds, stimulate discussion by adding in seeds which children may already be familiar with, in the context of food and eating, such as apple and tomato seeds, orange pips or garlic bulbs.

Follow the children's direction of investigation and facilitate their learning through well timed questions linked to their path of discovery. For example:

Which seed could be the heaviest? How could we find out?

How does it feel?

I wonder what might grow from a tiny seed. How could we find out?

If the path of discovery leads children to planting the seeds, take a photograph of the seed or encourage children to sketch and label the different seeds to attach to the pots.

Links to Early Learning Goals

CLL: *Use simple statements and questions often linked to gestures*
Use talk to organise, sequence and clarify thinking, ideas, feelings and events

KUW: *Investigate objects and materials by using all of their senses as appropriate*
Ask questions about why things happen and how things work
Find out about, and identify some features of living things, objects and events they observe

Best foot forward

Many young children are often fascinated by shoes and different footwear.

Provide a basket or box containing a selection of different footwear, sit back and observe what happens!

Resources

◆ Large box or basket

◆ Selection of footwear: baby shoes, lace ups, flip flops, slippers, different heel heights, Wellington boots, football boots…

◆ Different sizes of shoe boxes

Observe and note:

◆ How children make links with their previous experiences and share these with their friends.

◆ The words they use to describe sizes of shoes, especially when trying them on!

◆ The language children use to describe the style, colour, patterns and differences between shoes.

◆ If children order the shoes in anyway. Do they pair them up? How do they count the pairs?

◆ If children attempt to fasten / unfasten the shoes.

Questions to consider

Extend children's thinking through questions such as:

I wonder who they belong to?

Why do they wear them?

When do they wear them?

What if… The ballet dancer had Wellington boots?

What if… The footballer had ballet shoes?

Further learning opportunities can be facilitated by discussing and providing resources to:

◆ print patterns from the soles of the different shoes

◆ stimulate mixing and matching of footwear to dressing up clothes

◆ explore socks, which socks belong to which shoes?

◆ discuss safety footwear and clothing

Include a selection of other shoes and stories and see how the children sort and classify their choices.

The book area could easily accommodate the shoe theme! Can the children match items of footwear to a familiar story?

Suggested stories to link with footwear

Flipper – *Dougal's deep sea diary*
Welly Boot – *Percy the Park Keeper*
Glitzy slipper – *Cinderella*
Large boot – *Jack and the Beanstalk*
Baby Shoe – *The Baby Catalogue*

Links to Early Learning Goals

CLL: Use talk, actions and objects to recall and relive past experiences (Development matters)
Use talk to organise, sequence and clarify thinking, ideas, feelings and events.
Interact with others, negotiating plans and activities and taking turns in conversation
KUW: Look closely at similarities, patterns and change
PSRN: Sort familiar objects to identify their similarities and differences, making choices and justifying decisions

A hole lot of fun!

Children just love exploring holes of all different shapes and sizes. Providing a wide range of everyday items that allow children to explore the function and possibilities of holes could prove popular.

Resources

Everyday items with holes: Colander, sieve, slotted spoon, garlic press, tea strainer, salt cellar, straws, apple corer, shower head, cardboard tubes, pipes, watering can, plastic funnel, etc.

Book Area: Stories with holes! *The Very Hungry Caterpillar* by Eric Carle, *Peepo!* by Janet and Allan Ahlberg.

Writing Area: Hole-punchers, string, shaped paper with holes e.g. cheese shaped paper with holes, mini books with holes – replicating the style of books in the book corner.

Outdoor Area: Information books on animals that live in holes / burrows. Binoculars and notepads, spades, hand tools, nets and camouflage netting.

Questions to consider

What could it be?

How could we find out?

How could you use it?

What are the holes for?

The holey items could be explored in many different ways. Here are just a few ideas:

◆ Use coloured water, jugs and funnels to observe the speed and flow of water passing through.

◆ Make a concoction of fine and chunky items to sieve and sort e.g. flour and lentils or sand and jewels.

◆ Squeeze playdoh through the holes – great for the garlic press!

◆ Make vegetable soup and serve it using both a slotted spoon and a ladle. What's different? Why?

Links to Early Learning Goals

PD: Use a range of small and large objects
Handle tools, objects, construction and malleable materials safely and with increasing control

CD: Express and communicate their thoughts and feelings by using a widening range of materials and suitable tools (First part of ELG)

KUW: Investigate objects and materials by using all of their senses as appropriate
Ask questions about why things happen and how things work

CLL: Use talk to organise, sequence and clarify thinking, ideas, feelings and events

Gripping Fun!

Everyday pegs, used for hanging out the washing, are a source of amazement and fascination, and challenge children to explore the possibilities that this simple everyday item has to offer.

Resources

A simple washing line and a basket of pegs can create a whole host of questions for young inquisitive minds.

Pegs come in so many different shapes and sizes. Children will really call upon their fine motor skills as they examine different types of pegs such as wooden dolly pegs, large and small pegs, tiny pegs (used for card making), soft close rubbery pegs and novelty shaped pegs (smiley faces or penguins!)

Questions to consider

After children have had time and space to test the powers of pegs, the careful use of questioning can extend learning and development and promote higher order thinking.

I wonder… What would happen if we had something really heavy to peg up?

What would happen if a big gust of wind came along?

Can you say which peg is better? That's interesting; tell me about your idea?

How could we dry the animals? (selection of soft toys and hard small world figures)

As children become experts in using pegs and washing lines in both the indoor and outdoor environment, a variety of resources and activities could extend children's explorations and learning:

◆ Provide a wide range of fabrics, from silk ribbon to Hessian sacks, for children to investigate textures, patterns and colours. Are any fabrics more difficult to peg up?

◆ Washing clothes and fabrics in a range of sizes from dolls clothes to adults clothes.

◆ How long would they take to dry? Where will they dry the quickest? How could we find out? How do the children sort items on the washing line? Smallest to biggest, colours, etc.

◆ Read and share stories with a washing line theme such as *Mrs Mopple's washing line* by Anita Hewett, *Washing Line* by Jez Alborough or *Walter's Windy Washing Line* by Neil Griffiths.

◆ Provide clothes shaped paper in the writing area and washing lines and pegs for children to peg up their mark making and drawings.

Links to Early Learning Goals

PSED: Persist for extended periods of time at an activity of their choosing
Continue to be interested, excited and motivated to learn

CLL: Interact with others, negotiating plans and activities and taking turns in conversation
Enjoy listening to and using spoken and written language, and readily turn to it in their play and learning
Sustain attentive listening, responding to what they have heard with relevant comments, questions or actions
Begin to make patterns in their experience through linking cause and effect, sequencing, ordering and grouping (Development Matters)

PD: Manipulate materials to achieve a planned effect (Development Matters)
Use a range of small and large equipment

Wash and Scrub up!

Bringing together a range of brushes makes you realise just how many different sorts of brushes we use in everyday life and take for granted! Brushes come in all different shapes and sizes and are very tactile, each set of bristles just demands feeling and fingering.

Resources

You will need a set of brushes that could include: toothbrush, washing up brush, nail brush, scrubbing brush, shoe brush, hair brush (round and flat), bottle brush, pastry brush, paintbrush (selection of sizes), cosmetic brushes, shaving brush or back/bath brush.

Observe and note

Children will naturally explore and investigate the wide selection of brushes.

Make a note of the language used to describe the brushes or their uses; do the children use them to make marks or patterns? Do they transport the brushes to different areas and use them for different purposes? Is one type of brush popular in a particular area? Are all the shoe brushes being used for mark making in the foam?

As well as having a central brush selection, add brushes to a variety of resources and activities – What do the children do with the brushes? How do they use them?

- Paints, paper and toothbrushes and shoe-brushes
- Sand, shells and cosmetic brushes
- Water tray – bottles and bottle brushes
- Café – washing up brushes
- Wide selection of buckets and brushes in the outdoor area
- Hairdressers – bowls of water, dolls and hairbrushes
- Items for cleaning e.g. small world toys, cups, plates and nail brushes or washing up brushes
- Items buried in soil – Can the children use brushes to discover them?

Place different brushes with different resources around the setting over several days. Do children discover and invent new uses for them?

The story *Traction Man* by Mini Grey illustrates a scrubbing brush which comes to life and features throughout the story.

Can children create their own scrubbing brush creature? What story could their creature be in? What does he like doing?

Questions to consider

I see you are cleaning. Which brush is the best?

What could you use this brush for?

Have you seen these brushes before? What were they used for?

What do you use brushes for at home?

Links to Early Learning Goals

PSED: Be confident to try new activities, initiate ideas and speak in a familiar group

CLL Interact with others, negotiating plans and activities and taking turns in conversation

CLL: Enjoy listening to and using spoken language in their play and learning

CLL: Extend their vocabulary, exploring the meanings and sounds of new words

CLL: Use talk to organise, sequence and clarify thinking, ideas, feelings and events

PSRN: Use language such as 'circle' or 'bigger' to describe the shape and size of solids

PD: Use a range of small and large equipment

Learners as Experts –

further development of questioning skills

Learners as Experts –

further development of questioning skills

We know that through engaging and capturing children's imagination they develop a real sense of ownership over their activities and the direction in which their learning takes. Treating and respecting children as experts can really boost their confidence and empower them to confidently question and solve problems.

Children love receiving mail, letters and messages just for them; these are powerful tools for capturing children's interests and imagination. The following case studies show how children's learning and questioning can spiral into the exciting unknown, through communication aimed at recognising their skills and expertise and asking for further assistance.

Case Study 1– A new house for Rabbit

On a windy Thursday morning, the secretary arrived with a brown envelope with a leaf rubbing on the back. It was addressed to the group. The pre-briefed secretary announced, 'I think this must be for you'.

The children were gathered together when the speculation started; a huge amount of questions were raised by the children, of which, nearly all suggestions and answers were offered by their peers. Some of the questions were:

Did Mrs Smith (secretary) *send it to us?*

Who is it from?

Is it more bills? (Great prior knowledge of mail that arrives at home!)

Does it smell?! (Prompt sniffing of envelope by lots of children!)

How did it get here and how did they know our name?

One eager boy shouts, 'Let's open it!' as the children rip open the envelope.

They unravel the A3 size letter which reads:

> The Large Oak
> Woodland Way
> Forest View Park
> 123
>
> Dear Butterflies,
>
> We really need your help. Last night there was a terrible storm and poor Rabbit's burrow collapsed. Luckily, Rabbit is fine as she was visiting her friend Badger at the time.
>
> But she is very sad that she no longer has somewhere to live.
>
> Please could you help us with some ideas of how to build Rabbit a new house?
>
> We cannot wait to see and hear about all your ideas.
>
> Love from
>
> Percy the Park Keeper and all the animals

Shared reading of the unexpected letter provided a wonderful opportunity for the children to be fully involved in the reading process and for the practitioner to utilise their curiosity to predict why the sender may be writing to them.

As children used contextual and phonetic clues, along with their own prior knowledge of letters, the enthusiasm was astounding (if only this could be bottled!). Children were buzzing with ideas, as individual as their personalities.

All four themes of the EYFS merged, as the children took their role as experts very seriously, and set about to investigate, solve and reply to the problem posed to them.

With a huge variety of plans, structures and verbal ideas gathered it was time to respond to Percy's letter.

'How will we let Percy know all of our wonderful ideas?'

The children questioned each others' ideas, 'How would you know the rocket had taken the letter?' 'Does Percy have e-mail?' 'Does your Nanny know where he lives?' The combination of questioning and well-timed adult intervention led the children's thinking to a much deeper level.

Children were busily engaged in a variety of communication activities including filming one another verbally sharing their ideas, photographing their structures, placing their design drawings in envelopes, composing letters and notes, e-mailing their thoughts (after creating an e-mail address for him!) and creating invitations for Rabbit to come and stay at their homes!

Key workers worked alongside children to ensure they had both the support and resources to send their ideas in their preferred method.

The following week when children arrived in the morning there was a large 'Thank You' balloon on the fence outside. Children were questioning their parents, practitioners and friends as to the reason behind the balloon?

All was revealed when the children came in to find a large (stuffed!) rabbit sitting comfortably in a small chair with a tea set and, of course, an individual reply to all the ideas received!

The children felt like real experts as Rabbit individually responded and thanked the children for their ideas and very clever thinking.

A Unique Child	Each child followed their chosen path of enquiry and investigation, based on the question asked of them in the initial letter. No two children undertook identical activities and posed the same questions. Children developed confidence as they shared their ideas in small groups and used a myriad of tools and resources to communicate their thoughts and answers to both their own questions and the questions of others.
Positive Relationships	Key workers gained a deeper understanding of children's thought processes, prior knowledge and experiences. Using this understanding enabled practitioners to carefully plan next steps to develop children's skills across all areas.
Enabling Environments	Rich environments equipped with resources for children to independently access and tackle the task in hand. Using both indoor and outdoor areas to full effect some of the resources included: large scale paper and card, chunky marker pens, paints, woodland puppets, play dough, sticks, leaves, pine cones, straws, reclaimed materials, fabrics, construction materials, non-fiction books on buildings, construction blocks, hard hats, toolkits, clipboards, 'Percy the Park Keeper' books, selection of books on rabbits and toy rabbits.
Learning and Development	Children immersed themselves in using their expertise to help Rabbit. All areas of Learning and Development were interwoven as the children questioned, explored, created, discussed, collaborated, reviewed, refined, shared and communicated their findings to a range of audiences.

Case Study 2 – Jack needs our expertise

Following several weeks of practical activities linked to plants and growth, children had gained lots of experience in planting seeds, bulbs and established plants, in both indoor and outdoor areas. Many stories with a growth and plant theme had been shared, discussed, re-enacted, re-told and re-read.

Some of the popular stories included: *Jack and the Beanstalk*; *The Enormous Turnip*; *Jasper's Beanstalk* by Mick Inkpen; *Titch* by Pat Hutchins; *Jim and the Beanstalk* by Raymond Briggs; *The Tiny Seed* by Eric Carle; *In Wibbly's Garden* by Mick Inkpen.

The children were beginning to show real expertise as they actively shared their knowledge, through helping story characters with problems and questions during shared story sessions, acting out their own stories and helping customers in a garden centre role-play with advice and recommendations.

A precariously placed leaf shape had been left balancing on the top of the interactive whiteboard; it was carefully placed so that when the door to the outdoor area opened, it would fall onto the floor!

Right on cue, when the children were gathered together sharing their daily news, the door was opened and the leaf floated down. This caused great excitement as the children instantly became intrigued and offered their thoughts and ideas, including, 'It's windy!' 'It's raining paper!' 'It's not real!' 'It's from Laura's sunflower!' (The tallest growing sunflower outside!)

As the leaf landed it was noticed, 'It says something!' The children were itching to decode the message on the leaf – it had just one word,

HELP

A small group of children near the leaf supported one another, and with their combined phonic and blending, they decoded the message and excitedly shared this with the rest of the group.

Speculation began over whom the leaf was from and what help might be needed. A wide range of ideas and suggestions were shared, discussed and considered. The caretaker arrived at the door with two more leaves and announced, 'These were just by the door outside, do you know anything about them?'

A rush of excitement spread as the children eagerly awaited the next instalment of the message!

'I told you it was Spiderman, he flies outside, that's why they were there.'

'Perhaps it's more of Laura's sunflower?'

'Who needs help?'

'Does it say?'

'Can I see?'

Together, the leaves were carefully analysed and predictions about the content were made. Jack had already identified that they were from him, he had seen his name at the bottom!

The message was jointly read by the children with the support of a practitioner.

Leaf One

You all seem to know so much about plants and growing things. I really need your help...

Leaf Two

...The beanstalk isn't strong enough to hold me up for much longer. I keep hearing it creaking and it's beginning to bend. What can I do? From Jack

After identifying who had sent the messages, the children were only too pleased to assist!

Children dispersed across all areas of the setting and began putting their ideas into action. As key workers listed and noted, it later transpired that children had immediately been drawn to their preferred style of learning in order to help Jack.

A large number of children remained focused on finding a solution for Jack for the rest of the afternoon and the following day. Key workers supported learners, by encouraging evaluation of their designs and creations. Evaluating often led to refinement as new areas, additions or ideas were explored and tested. Capitalising on children's eagerness to discuss and show their ideas, regular opportunities were provided for children to share their current developments with the rest of the group. The communication skills demonstrated by the children were amazing, children actively listened to the ideas of others, processed the information and asked questions to gain a greater understanding and find out further details.

It was apparent that children were learning from one another and imitating the ideas they had seen from a friend into their own design, creation or story.

A large stem was used as the means for transporting all of the ideas back to Jack, individual leaves were attached which held photographs, drawings, messages and pictures of the ideas and solutions to his problems.

The next day a very large leaf shape was left next to the stem and shared reading together discovered the following message:

I am so tired I have been up nearly all night, reading all of your wonderful ideas!

Thank you so much – they have really helped me. I am going to be looking out for your hands coming to rescue me, I will also try throwing down some heavy things and if they don't work I might try the idea of flying away on the hen.

Thank you again so much – I am going to read your ideas again after my golden eggs on toast tonight.

Love from Jack and a wobbly beanstalk.

The children beamed and showed a genuine sense of pride and achievement in their diverse and individual solutions to Jack's problems.

A Unique Child	Each child was able to respond to Jack's message using their own unique preferred style of learning. Children chose their own areas within the learning environment and it was evident that they had selected their preferred areas, with the usual residents of the writing den busy replying to Jack whilst the outdoor crew were busy trying to construct a tower out of boxes to rescue Jack!
Positive Relationships	The initial discussions gave opportunity to reinforce listening to and respecting the ideas of others, along with, promoting asking questions to find out more about individual ideas. Children are able to independently choose how to communicate their ideas.
Enabling Environments	Children feel confident and secure to explore the learning environment, being able to test, apply and demonstrate their ideas. The environment is equipped with resources and materials to enable and encourage children to explore, question, consolidate and develop new skills. For example Problem Solving Toolkits containing a variety of tape measures, rulers, string, pencils, notebooks and calculators were transported outside and used to help the group of children busy designing and building a tower to reach Jack.
Learning and Development	A busy, purposeful buzz filled the air, as a myriad of activities and solutions developed. A snapshot showed children exploring the tall sunflowers to see how they stand up, writing replies to Jack, making a big tall stalk and leaves to replace the weak one, seeing who could paint the tallest beanstalk and re-telling the story of Jack and The Beanstalk with and without alternative endings, including the beanstalk collapsing!

Case Study 3 – Wizard's Worries

Magical and sparkly thoughts had been plentiful and evident, as children were busy dressing up being fairies and wizards. Spells had been created, practitioners were turned into frogs, and fairies were designing their fairy outfits!

Later in the morning, a note on the computer indicated 'You have mail'. After discussing this message with the children it become apparent that this was a familiar message, which indicated an e-mail had been sent. The e-mail (pre-prepared and sent) contained the following message:

From: Magicalmysteries@spellcity.co.uk
   To: Butterflies@thestreet.co.uk

Dear Butterflies,
We have a problem and wondered if you could help us with something?

Wizard Winston really needs to make a new potion to give him a magical power. Which magical power would be best?

We would love some of your fabulous ideas to help Winston.

Lots of sparkledust
From Starlight x

After several re-readings, together the information was distilled and the key question identified:

What is a magical power?

Children excitedly shared their thoughts with one another; together they unpicked the meaning of 'magical power' and shared their knowledge. As they shared their ideas and thoughts together as a group, the enormous range of children's prior fantasy knowledge became evident. Lively demonstrations, from Spiderman's web flinging and climbing to Flower Fairies being invisible, took place.

Which magical power is best? Scribing a list of the children's collective knowledge of magical powers emerged as the starting point for testing a range of powers. Powers were put to the test across the setting with exciting flying heroes play, writing with invisible ink and wands casting spells, whilst potion making was being put straight to the test too!

Children questioned and analysed the pros and cons of different powers, with the support of practitioners. The questions and thoughts covered all 6 levels of Bloom's Taxonomy, as these examples show:

Are magic powers real?

Can spiders spin real webs?

If my hands were magit (magnetic) would I stick to metal things?

I don't think Wizards are small.

Do wizards like being small or big?

I am going to use my wings to fly to Florida.

If I was a wizard… I would make spells to make me strong and lift cars and lorries.

Shrinking is no good cos you will get trod on!

As magic powers were decided upon and individual children had chosen their power, the job of creating the potions began! Bottles, jars, pots, funnels, sieves, mixing bowls, whisks, scoops, spoons and a huge array of materials from glitter to mud were accessible. Learners were engrossed in pouring, mixing, filling, discussing and describing their potions. Labels were created and attached and the results of drinking the potions were convincingly acted out. In groups, children showed everyone their potions and described the magic power they would give.

A large envelope was prepared for Winston with photographs of all of the children and their potions, and pictures or messages describing what magical powers their potion would bring.

An e-mail was sent to tell Winston, asking him to keep an eye out for the postman carrying a large envelope.

The following day a large wizard puppet sat on the carpet, complete with a potion bottle and an envelope addressed to the group. Together the group excitedly opened and read Winston's thank you card – he was going to test out all of the potions!

A Unique Child	Risks and potential hazards are considered as children discuss different magical powers. Children hook into magical powers according to their own interests, from designing extra large fairy wings to leaping off stacks of crates to test flying skills. Children confidently communicate their ideas in a variety of ways.
Positive Relationships	Children are supported to respect the ideas and opinions of others as the pros and cons of magical powers are discussed. Learning and development is shared with parents through a photographic display and individual learning records.
Enabling Environments	Creations, from magic spell sparkly slippers to magnet man's metal arms are created! Children are enabled by wide and varied resources to follow their own lines of enquiry and test out their unique and personalised ideas.
Learning and Development	◆ Generating ideas ◆ Collaboration ◆ Evaluating ◆ Exploring liquids and materials ◆ Mark making ◆ Speaking and Listening

Case study 4 – A visit from Jack Frost

Seasonal weather is just perfect for inspiring children to wonder, question and discover.

Here we see how a particularly chilly snap demanded investigating with the children leading their learning.

After a very small snowfall children were eager to build snowmen, snow children and snow ladies!

After scraping together enough snow to create four very small snow creations the children were bursting to share these with their parents and carers at the end of the session.

Sadly, the next day all that was left were the sticks and buttons that had been used to add detail. The children were really disappointed.

Building upon children's reactions and feelings through offering further investigation and understanding is crucial.

Children further explored the process of melting through ice play: freezing objects in ice, creating ice worlds – including adding glitter, sequins, flour, salt and other materials suggested and selected by themselves.

The children decided to leave outside overnight a variety of containers filled with different ice creations, they wanted to see if these would also disappear!

The next morning the following note was discovered hanging close to where they had left their ice creations:

I tried and tried to work my frosty magic on your lovely ice models, but it was just too warm last night. Is there anything you could do to keep your ice cold tonight?

Chilly wishes
Jack Frost

A small group of boys discovered the message from Jack Frost. Together they shared their ideas about the message.

'He melted them!'

'He's been here!'

'No – he makes stuff froze' (modelling a spiky statue)

'He didn't froze mine – the feather is all… yuck' (picking out a soggy feather from a small bowl)

The boys run around making spiky shapes and zapping one another with their ice guns.

As a child makes his 'froze' shape, he picks up another note from Jack Frost:

'No more snow it's all gone' he reads with his finger following the words left to right

'No… show…. A… A… Amber she knows numbers!'

The boys rush inside to find Amber (busy cutting, gluing and creating signs for her bedroom). The practitioner observes Amber's body language as her self-esteem escalates at her important job of helping the boys to decode the message. She carefully sounds out the words, blending when she can. (A true Learning Journey moment!)

A well-timed intervention from a practitioner asks the boys and Amber to share what they have found with the group.

Reading the note together provided a wonderful observation opportunity, as the practitioner noted children's individual contributions and knowledge of sounds, words and the reading process.

Children were buzzing with excitement and ideas to help keep the ice cold.

A lengthy discussion with them about putting the freezer outside demonstrated the children's wide and varied prior experiences (including seeing Dad's beer fridge in the garden at a BBQ!)

The children became engrossed in wrapping, posting, packing and exploring ice. Their ideas were never-ending and included putting an ice cube inside Teddy's jumper and packing and wrapping lots of ice cubes.

Making careful use of questioning, to encourage the children to share their ideas and clarify their thoughts, by asking 'Wow that looks interesting – Can you tell me about it?' Gave children the chance to share their thoughts and lead into their own questioning, 'Will it fall out?' 'Why did it get too warm?'

Allowing children the freedom and choice to move between the indoor and outdoor area is essential in enabling them to immediately test out their ideas and further develop their own questioning and reasoning skills and become absorbed in their activities.

'The outdoor space must be viewed as an essential teaching and learning environment which is linked with the learning that goes on inside, but with even greater status because it allows for children to learn through movement' Marjorie Ouvry

The continuation of activities from the previous day facilitated children's natural inquisitiveness and provided an opportunity for them to test out their own thoughts and ideas, as well as reflect and review their findings. (Bear in mind that sometimes questions from an adult can hinder a child's train of thought or their own thought processing.)

'Creating the right conditions for children to develop confidence in themselves as learners, explorers, discoverers and critical thinkers is vital in a rapidly changing world.' Primary National Strategy, Confident, Capable and Creative: supporting boys' achievements.

A Unique Child	Following their own path of enquiry children were able to devise, create and monitor their own investigations and find their own answers to their unique thoughts, ideas and questions. Children could access the activities based on their unique needs, like Amber, keen to use the writing implements to make signs to keep her little brother out of her bedroom!
Positive Relationships	Careful listening to children's discussions identified a new route to explore, involving parents and carers. Hearing one child tell his friends his Dad broke his leg in the snow, this opportunity was captured and the parent invited in to tell the children all about it! A wonderful snow safety discussion followed with the children telling the parent what he should have done!
Enabling Environments	The indoor and outdoor environments were equipped with wide and inviting resources, which children were able to select independently and supported them in following their own direction of learning. A varied selection of ice inspired resources available throughout the environment including: cold colour paints, spiky shaped paper, Jack Frost writing frames, jugs, bowls, lids, ice cube trays, large boxes, tin foil, fabric, plastic bags, assorted reclaimed boxes and containers.
Learning and Development	Children confidently used their current and prior understanding to pose questions and help Jack Frost solve his problem. Confidently they reasoned, questioned, constructed, communicated through written and spoken words, tested, investigated, predicted and summarised their thoughts and ideas.

An interview with...

using interviews to stimulate questioning

An interview with...

Using interviews to stimulate questioning

Interviewing a wide and varied range of people, including guest visitors, familiar adults (in and out of role), children, parents and professionals can be effective in stimulating learners to question. Questions can be used to find out more information, extend knowledge and understanding, satisfy or extend curiosity and imagination, as well as developing confidence and communication skills.

Who could you interview?

Actively seeking opportunities to bring in experts or professionals linked to areas of interests or a theme within the setting enhances the knowledge, skills and enthusiasm of many learners and enables each child to satisfy their own unique curiosities.

Interviewing Experts

An interview with a **Scuba Diver**

Inspired by the story *Dougal's Deep-sea Diary* by Simon Bartram, children had many questions, thoughts and ideas which they wanted to find out more about. Life under the sea permeated across all areas of learning and throughout the setting. As parents became aware of some of the questions the children wanted to find out, one parent had a friend who was a very keen scuba diver and had recently returned from a trip, complete with under the sea footage – just perfect!

A visit was arranged for two scuba divers to come in to be interviewed by the children and share their expertise – and they would be bringing along some equipment!

Excitement had been building as the children began considering some of the things that they wanted to find out. As soon as the children saw some of the equipment it triggered a huge amount of questions!

Our visiting scuba divers introduced themselves and were really interested in the under the sea displays, resources and learning evident in the environment and more so, young learners bubbling with knowledge and questions.

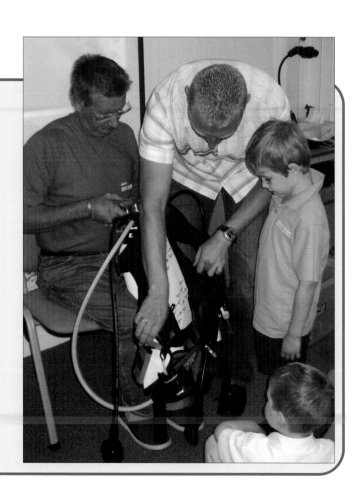

Practitioners encouraged and supported children to voice the questions that they had been asking during activities and investigations (the well prepared practitioners had scribed the questions with the children over a period of time in case they needed a little reminder). Some of the initial questions included:

What do octopus legs stick too?

Why didn't Dougal sink with his tank on?

Have you seen a shark?

Have you been bitten?

There was a true sense of awe and wonder as our experts answered many questions, supported by firsthand photographs, video footage, equipment and scars (from jellyfish stings!). Deeply absorbed in hearing tales from under the sea, learners quickly processed information and posed additional questions to further extend their knowledge and understanding. Each explanation to a question triggered more questions – the children were fascinated and engrossed in the replies to their questions. They were desperate to find out as much as they could.

The response to the simple question – Have you seen a shark? – triggered an abundance of further questions and a detailed, extensive discussion on jellyfish. The chidren requested several replays of seeing a jellyfish in action! There were squeals of delight as the jellyfish came towards the camera and complete disbelief as children discovered that jellyfish have no eyes, brains or bones! As children considered this new information and tried to make sense of it, many more questions followed.

Lots of activities and research investigations stemmed from interviewing our visitors. Learners were eager to make sense of all of the new information they had absorbed, and play was taken to a new dimension as children began to apply more technical vocabulary and share their knowledge. Here's just a snapshot of some of the comments heard as children were busily engaged in play activities:

'Quick, pull the cord my oxgin (oxygen) is running out!'

'The next boat leaves to go to the reef at 3 o'clock. You will have to take your tank off on the boat, would you like a ticket?'

'Watch out a stingy jellyfish is chasing you!'

'No he's not – he can't see me.' (reply to the above)

Children attached piping to the base of a large water container (being used as a tank) and make 'psssssssssssss' sounds:

'Let's get out of the water and fill up our tanks!'

Further research was undertaken to establish just how jellyfish function and live without a brain – deep and advanced thinking for 4 and 5 year olds!

Expert visitors provide a wonderful opportunity for extending children's knowledge, introducing different roles and specialisms and maybe even inspiring children to consider their future careers!

An interview with a **Pilot**

After lots of investigating and finding out about night time and nocturnal activities, many learners were wondering 'Why does it go dark?' and 'How does it go dark?' This complex question was initially tackled, using a tennis ball, an apple and a torch, to model the earth spinning and the sun shining. The children were fascinated, although left with even more thoughts about 'How does the earth spin?' Introducing the earth into children's learning initiated thoughts and questions about planets and if they were real. An inflatable solar system was sourced and provided a visual, big picture of night, day and space with the children.

From here questions and learning took a new direction as children became interested and curious about space. Who could we pose our questions too? One of the children had previously lived in America and had brought in pictures and information from NASA space centre. After chatting to the child's mum it transpired that her husband was serving at the local air base and had previously spent time training at Kennedy Space Centre and... he would be happy to come in and help to answer our questions!

Practitioners were amazed at the thought and effort that our visitor had put into preparing an image rich presentation for the children. The children were really excited about our visitor's air force uniform and as he introduced himself he explained the badges and logos on his uniform and the purpose behind the different pockets.

The questions the children had previously wanted to ask were soon forgotten as the big bag that arrived with our visitor demanded investigating! As vacuum packed space food, equipment and photographs were shared a myriad of questions were considered, posed and discussed. One child linked their learning back to when we had previously watched the first landing on the moon and used our bodies to move like astronauts and asked:

Why do you bounce in space?

The children were captivated as they learned our visitor had experienced being weightless in NASA's vomit comet – infectious laughter spread as the children saw images of adults 'floating' and heard about the meaning behind the name 'vomit comet'! The questions flowed and, again, the explanation to one question provided loads more!

Having real life experts visit a setting brings an air of excitement and magic. It can kindle learning unique to children's questions and interests, which could never be planned for, pre-determined or guessed. Feedback from parents and carers showed that children had gone home bursting with information and news. Parents commented, 'I never knew that!' 'He teaches us stuff these days!' 'He is certain he wants to be an astronaut now!'

Everyday experts in real-life familiar occupations fascinate children and often they already have a wealth of firsthand experience of these occupations to build upon.

An interview with a Cook

The children were all familiar with the work of the setting's cook. They would regularly interact with her when using the oven, fridge or freezer to house various creations, and of course, they would see her each day as she served lunch.

They relished the opportunity to interview the cook and were surprised that she was able to come out of the kitchen to talk to them!

Cooking had always proved to be a popular activity in this setting and the children often posed questions relating to cooking methods and recipes. After identifying that the cook may be the best person to help them find out more, questions and thoughts were gathered ready to ask the cook. Again, the pattern continued and the children (even though already familiar with seeing her) were intrigued by the cook's apron and hat. Many of the children offered different ideas about the purpose behind the apron and hat. Good hygiene practices were reinforced as their ideas were clarified by the cook.

A greater insight was gained into the busy, working kitchen through asking questions and sharing their thoughts. The questions showed that children were trying to make sense and build upon their own experiences with baking, with questions such as:

Why do things burn?

What do you do if you burn something?

Why can't you eat burnt things?

It was apparent that the sheer scale of the kitchen had been considered through the following questions:

How do you know how much to cook?

Why are your trays so big?

How many potatoes do you cook?

The cook's responses seemed to instantly satisfy the inquisitive minds, but many children were still pondering on some of the answers after she had left.

Arranging a visit to see the cook in action throughout the remainder of the week gave children the chance to process their thoughts, analyse the information and, if needed, ask further questions.

The opportunity to see the equipment and tools inspired children to create and run their own play kitchens and restaurants.

An interview with a **Gardener**

Green fingers were tingling, as eager young gardeners tended to the vegetable bed, tubs and pots in their setting's outdoor area.

Although, strange things were happening… Green potatoes, leaves with holes in, onions with wiggly grubs in… Oh no! What could we do? Of course, let's find an expert – we could ask them about our problems and show them our gardens!

It was decided that the local allotments may be a good place to start. A discussion with the children about allotments resulted in one of the children sharing with us, 'My next door neighbour has one and goes there with his spade'. Great! A visit was arranged and the child's Mum accompanied her neighbour – giving a hand to carry a few tools and vegetables in!

A tour of the setting's gardens gave the children an opportunity to share their gardens and the things they had been busy doing. The children were bursting to share all of the 'problems' with our expert, 'Look there are the leaves with holes' and 'the tatos (potatoes) were all green'.

Our expert was great at listening to the children's questions and then encouraging them to gather near to the plant or area in discussion and explaining what had happened and what could be done about it.

Our expert showed them his gardening tools and the children made excellent predictions about their possible uses. They were able to identify many of the vegetables and were now really desperate to grow their own pumpkins!

The questions flowed naturally, enhanced by being in the outdoor environment. The snapshot of questions below gives an idea of the vast range of questions:

Have you really got green fingers?

Can pumpkins plode (explode)*?*

Do caterpillars really eat cake? (Linking to **The Very Hungry Caterpillar**!)

Can you eat green potatoes?

The children were eager to put some of our gardener's ideas into action! The following days showed a huge increase in the number of children choosing the outdoor area. Observations showed: Individual children taking on the role of expert and imitating our visitor, groups of children designing caterpillar traps (to trap and keep as pets), using spades and rakes imitating the skills of our visitor, children making signs to 'keep off the garden' and watering the tubs and pots. As new questions arose, children confidently gave answers and predictions, inspired by our 'green fingered' visitor.

Experts from familiar occupations, such as police officers, shopkeepers and nurses, can be invaluable in germinating children's initial seeds of thought, building upon their existing knowledge and identifying any misconceptions they might have about certain jobs. By having real-life experts available to answer children's questions and listen to their thoughts and ideas learning and motivation is enhanced.

An interview with Firefighters

Observations were showing that many children were displaying a keen interest in firefighters and the work of the fire brigade. Arranging a visit from firefighters at the onset of children's displayed enthusiasm, motivated and empowered children to lead and instigate exciting firefighter activities and stories, rich with learning and development opportunities.

A prompt visit was arranged with the local fire station, who were more than happy to visit and use the opportunity to also reinforce fire safety.

A message arrived that our firefighters were waiting in the car park. Gasps and wows filled the air as the children noticed that they had travelled in the fire engine!

The priceless, firsthand opportunity to explore the fire engine answered so many questions, but also posed so many more. As children discovered the engine's tools, hoses and ladders their questioning began to show a great deal of thought, with questions such as:

What happens if two people call at the same time?

Can the hose reach high fires?

If you get dressed in the fire engine, do you wear a seatbelt?

Why do you have different coloured helmets?

The most popular request being – *Can we see the lights again?*

In the quieter indoor environment, the firefighters skilfully weaved fire safety advice and guidance into the discussions and further questions. As children reflected on their visit to the engine, further questions were asked to clarify their thoughts. The question; 'Why are there no girl fireman?' ignited the most wonderful discussions! Many of the children were absolutely amazed to hear that there are women firefighters, again triggering lots of questions such as, 'Can they climb ladders?' 'Do they wear the same clothes?' This provided a wonderful opportunity to dispel gender stereotyping.

Fire stations and call centres were constructed; firefighters bravely tackled many wide ranging emergencies, all role-played with conviction!

Thanking visitors can provide the ideal chance to reflect and evaluate on the information and learning, which may stem from their visit. Photographs, pictures, cards, messages on themed shaped paper, are just some of the ways to thank visitors and share some of the things that may have been discovered since. Another great way to consolidate learning is to create a mini book showing the activities, explorations and learning that followed from their visit.

Fictitious Characters

Interviewing fictitious characters brings about an opportunity to develop imagination, analyse characters and events and synthesise (link) with their own ideas. (See Blooms Taxonomy.)

An interview with
Jolly Pete the Pirate

Following several weeks of learning about pirates, solving pirate problems, making pirate ships, discovering treasure and hearing pirate tales, a visit from 'Jolly Pete' was planned. Jolly Pete had previously sent a message, in a bottle, to ask if he could pop in the next day as he would be sailing by.

Anticipation and suspense grew as children questioned:

Who is Pete?

Where will he leave his pirate ship?

Will he have a parrot? They can bite!

I bet he's not real.

Is he from the story?

We're gonna show him our ship and make him walk the plang (plank)!

The arrival of Pete was a great source of humour as children identified they knew who it really was – Jolly Pete was in fact one of their familiar key workers, dressed as a pirate, complete with moustache, albeit a wobbly one!

A lively Jolly Pete explained he was sailing past and wanted to hear all of their pirate ideas. Pirate knowledge, ideas, games and stories were shared. Jolly Pete was very impressed, especially as only two pirates had walked the plank!

As children relaxed into Jolly Pete's role they began to question his existence as a pirate, 'Why doesn't your parrot fly away?' 'What do you eat?' 'Where do you keep your canon balls?'

Jolly Pete was very tactful at turning the questions around and gathering the children's ideas and perspectives on what they would have done, or where they would have stored their items and why. Food became a hot topic of conversation, the children were adamant that everything was always stored in sacks and that mice would eat lots of things – great knowledge!

Just before he left, Jolly Pete viewed the children's large and small scale pirate ships, paintings, life size pirates, parrots and canon ball machines! This gave children a real sense of value and achievement as he marvelled at their wonderful thinking, ideas and creations. 'I think I have made some new shipmates!' he exclaimed, as the children beamed and evaluated, 'He thinks our ship is great!'

Jolly Pete's visit inspired children to create their own messages in bottles, bake biscuits (and find a way of keeping them where mice couldn't nibble them) and create their own rigging for climbing. Observing the questions, interests and opinions of the children whilst interacting with Jolly Pete allowed practitioners to plan activities, resources and opportunities for further exploration.

An interview with
Humpty Dumpty

A chance to interview the character himself! This traditional nursery rhyme has always conjured up images, problems and solutions, in the minds of children and adults alike.

As Humpty, dressed in a large painted cardboard egg and bow tie, spontaneously drops in one morning, the children are instantly amused – especially when they know Humpty is really one of their practitioners.

Humpty asks the group, 'Do you know my rhyme?' Enthusiastically the children sing Humpty Dumpty together. The questions instantly began without any prompting or encouragement. (Sometimes you can think for the children too much – a bank of prompts had been planned.) The first question, 'How come you are fixed?' led to some fabulous ideas!

Humpty was very convincing as he consolidated children's knowledge of the rhyme by asking: 'Who couldn't put me back

Humpty was very convincing as he consolidated children's knowledge of the rhyme by asking: 'Who couldn't put me back together again?' Ideas were then gathered by asking, 'Well I have a great new shell now!' 'What do you think happened next?' Unique and magical responses included, 'They took you to the hospital' 'You grew a new shell' 'They found glue and glued you back' 'You borrowed a shell' and 'The wall really had a trampoline underneath'.

Children questioned Humpty Dumpty's knowledge of safety and his decision making through questions such as: 'Why did you sit on the wall?' 'Did you know it was tall?' and 'Where was your mum?' This gave a clear indication of the children's current level of assessing risks, especially as they began giving Humpty advice about what he could have done instead! Spontaneity can often be very memorable for young children, some years later children still reminisce 'Remember, when you were Humpty?'

'Memorable activities lead to memorable learning.'
Robin Hammerton HMI

Mrs Christmas, The Fairy Godmother and a Giant have all proved to be excellent fictitious characters for inspiring children to question, imagine and wonder.

Parent Partnership

Parent Partnership

The powerful partnership between home and early years settings is crucial in establishing a solid, emotionally secure and positive base on which each child's future educational experiences will be built.

'Parents are children's first and most enduring educators. When parents and practitioners work together in early years settings, the results have a positive impact on children's development and learning.' EYFS 2008

An open, honest, valued and respected relationship between home and setting is essential for supporting a child's transition into a new setting, learning new skills and continuing their learning journey, which will last a lifetime.

It is crucial that practitioners find out as much as possible about each unique child and their families. Placing time and importance on finding out about children's favourite activities, dislikes, past nursery or day care experiences, individual needs, family, pets, home, friends and interests will prove invaluable in developing an understanding of the journey of learning the child has already experienced.

How can parents support questioning?

It is really important for parents to understand the types of questions that their child will be thinking and finding out about during their time in the setting and the impact these can have on their child's learning and development.

Offering a range of opportunities for parents to discover more about questions to stimulate learning and development can help to secure and maintain positive partnerships.

Parents and carers could find out more about questions to support learning through:

- spending time observing and interacting in sessions with an opportunity to follow up by chatting to practitioners

- hearing examples of types of questions in all workshops, for example – reading, outdoor learning or healthy eating

- attending evening presentations/information sessions

- newsletters and posters

- daily/weekly snippets on message boards

- question of the week/month e.g. What if… you could fly? Invite parents to chat with their child and record their findings and ideas if they wish to. Findings could be shared through pictures, words, models, physical exploration, films, magazine clippings – the list is endless!

- encouraging parents to ask their child: What questions have you asked today?

- testing out 'I wonder…' questions at home e.g. I wonder why Bob chose to be a builder?

Questioning in Action!

'Parents should review their children's progress regularly and contribute to their child's learning and development record.' EYFS

Capture children's questions, thoughts, ideas and responses to stimuli and add these to their individual learning records. Individual learning records are essential not only for capturing a child's learning journey and reviewing and planning the next steps for their development but also for sharing and celebrating their individual learning journeys with parents and carers.

Encourage parents and carers to record children's ideas, thoughts and questions in the learning record, just as maybe they would record that their child counted five objects. What questions have they asked? What have they been wondering about?

Parent Expertise

Parents and carers can enhance the provision within a setting enormously. Seeking the views and opinions of parents can promote evaluation, research and often refinement of current practice and policies.

Parents play a huge part in helping to satisfy children's curiosity and develop their knowledge and understanding of the world around them. Parents bring with them rich and diverse skills and experiences that lead to memorable activities and sessions with children. So use a message board, notes, and flyers from the children or pictures of the current questions, thoughts or problems to ask for any parental help or ideas!

A Year One child was really intrigued with the cement mixer she had seen on-site (building work being undertaken). She observed the cement mixer a great deal and was especially keen to see what happened when the mixer stopped. She asked, 'How come the cement doesn't fall out when it goes round?' This wonderful question stimulated some insightful discussions and led to some very messy and complex experiments! Displaying the question for parents to see at home time enabled them to chat with their child on the way home and find out more about their learning. One child's uncle was a builder and was pestered by his niece to come in and tell the class about mixers!

Inviting and encouraging parents and family visitors in to the setting to share their expertise and experiences can enthuse and inspire children to imitate, question, respect and understand.

Developing positive, informal relationships with parents and families will enable practitioners to be aware of the skills and expertise they have and reassure parents and families who may feel a little daunted at the prospect of coming into school, talking and sharing their skills and knowledge with a group of young children.

Here are just a few of the visitors that have left lasting memories with the children who were fortunate enough to hear their tales and share their knowledge: A Jamaican grandmother telling traditional Jamaican tales and rhymes, a new mum bathing her baby, a Rabbi re-enacting a Passover meal, a paramedic talking about his job and reinforcing keeping safe, a mum from Indonesia sharing her knowledge and experiences, a traveller grandfather who made wagons, a Turkish aunt cooking traditional Turkish cuisine with the children, a Cantonese family sharing customs and beliefs (and a return visit at Chinese New Year to celebrate and support cooking activities) and a dad with a broken leg talking about his x-ray and experience of his leg being plastered.

Parent partnerships should be shared and celebrated – displaying photographs of parents visiting the setting, helping at a party or reading stories to children, places high value on the partnership.

Reciprocate with gestures to say 'Thanks' – cakes or biscuits made by the children along with a picture or letter of thanks shows appreciation and really adds value to the contributions from parents, carers and families.

Why not share thanks and celebrations with the wider community by inviting the local press to events such as parties or sunflower measuring days?

A little bit of the setting going home…

Not quite the furniture or brickwork, but looking for opportunities to send home resources, discovery projects and familiar toys can strengthen partnerships between home and school.

Capitalising on opportunities to mirror investigations in the setting and home can deepen children's learning and development. The thought, 'I wonder how big sunflowers can really grow?' resulted in children planting and caring for sunflowers within their setting. Children designed and illustrated information leaflets telling parents all about their investigation. Then, seeds, yoghurt pots and a small bag of compost were given to each child to take home and do a spot of planting with their parent or carer.

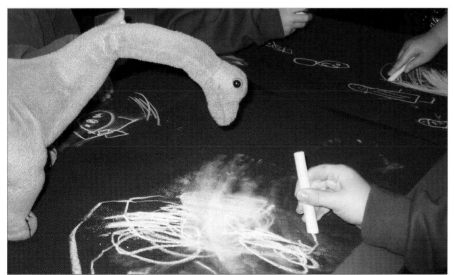

Tales of sunflowers came flooding in ranging from 'The dog knocked it over!' to 'It's too big now can I bring it back?'

Vice versa, encouraging children to bring in a little piece of home to share with their friends and key workers can help children to settle and develop a strong link between home and their nursery or school. Photographs, favourite toys, leaflets of places they have been, postcards from holidays or a favourite story are perfect for building confidence to share and communicate about their unique and individual home lives.

Personalising Learning

Personalising Learning

They (children) don't learn at an even rate. They learn in spurts and the more interested they are in what they are learning, the faster these spurts are likely to be.

Studies have shown that when children feel control and ownership over their learning they display higher levels of motivation, deeper engagement, an increase in original ideas and a desire to want to learn. Making learning irresistible to children will support children to becoming enthusiastic, flexible and confident learners for life.

Questions can be used as a powerful tool to help children gain control and direction over both their individual learning and the collective learning of a group.

'Helping children to think of questions which they want to find out the answers to is important. They will find it easier and more meaningful to try and find out the answers if they themselves have asked the questions.' Anna Craft

There are a wide range of strategies, frameworks and tools to help learners structure and release their thoughts and ideas.

One framework that has proved really useful in helping to personalise learning across all phases of education is the use of KWFL grids. I first came across the use of KWFL grids in 2004 when Gill Hubble – an international consultant in learning and thinking – shared this tool, along with many other approaches, to develop whole school thinking, at a conference in Suffolk.

Over the past five years, I have experimented with the use of KWFL grids firsthand, across the Foundation Stage, Key Stage One and Key Stage Two. The results have been enlightening and have proven invaluable in getting to know the areas, topics, interests and passions of learners within my care.

The KWFL structure uses four key questions to open up a topic or new area of discovery, enabling learners to identify the elements that really hook them in:

K	W	F	L
What do we know?	What do we want to know?	How could we find out?	What have we learned?

K
What do we know?

It is crucial to establish what children already know about a topic of learning, at the very beginning. This opening question could be:

- Broad such as – What do you know about life under the sea?

- Theme focussed, for example a mythical focus – What do you know about mermaids?

- Information focussed – What do you know about sea creatures?

- A detailed focus – What do you know about crabs?

The choice of questions will be dependent on the purpose: Is it to plan an afternoon's session or establish the direction over a period of weeks or evaluate a series of previous learning experiences?

By sharing what they already know, children are actively engaged in learning from one another. Giving children the opportunity to share their knowledge and understanding, in a variety of ways, builds their confidence and self-esteem.

It is also a crucial chance for practitioners to capture children's current understanding and identify any early misconceptions.

It was proven just how powerful this method can be when establishing what a Year One class knew about 'Growing Plants'. I realised that they already knew the names of all the parts of a plant, the functions of many parts and the most and least effective conditions for growing plants, all of which I had 'planned' to cover over the following weeks!

The next question, 'What do you want to find out?' re-established the planning of learning activities and skills based on children's identified areas of interest, which were far more advanced and included questions such as, 'Why are leaves never blue?'

Involving children in planning their learning makes them feel valued and gives them a sense of ownership over their learning. Learning in which children are an integral part of planning and driving, for real reasons, can have far greater outcomes than a pre-determined curriculum that is 'delivered' and seen by children as something that is 'done to them'.

Just a few ways in which children could communicate what they already know:

- Verbally sharing with individuals, small or large groups.

- Drawing pictures maybe on relevant shaped paper e.g. plant pot shaped.

- Using written words and marks.

- Filming information 'news reports'.

- Voice recording materials (a range is available from TTS).

- Scribing their ideas (with your help) onto a mind map, to be added to as investigations unfold.

W
What do we want to know?

It is here that the most exciting, intriguing and original questions and thoughts come to light. Identifying what children want to know gives children a chance to voice their curiosity and tap into the areas that they are interested and intrigued by. These are often the most gruesome areas or areas of extremeness, just like high scoring top trump cards are the most sought after!

A young child's mind poses questions which as adults we could never 'plan' to cover. For example, when thinking of our bodies here are just a few of the questions posed by Year Three children:

◆ How do you speak?

◆ Why does my arm sometimes taste salty if I lick it?

◆ What are we made of?

◆ How do you get blood in your lips?

◆ How many bones are in your muscles?

◆ How much veins go through your body?

This snapshot gives an insight into the thoughts of the children and instantly shows the content of learning over the coming weeks.

F
How can we find out?

This question is vital for developing resourcefulness and equipping children with the skills to know how and where to find things out, seek more information, make contact with experts or professionals and engage further in a topic or area that appeals to them. This is a crucial skill for life, which as adults we actively use, refine and apply every single day when we need to know how to find directions to somewhere, the telephone number for an advice line or how to keep slugs off cabbages.

Involving children in planning how to find out the answers to the questions that have been raised will give them greater ownership of their learning and draw upon and extend their current research and resource skills.

'How can we find out?' may involve:

◆ Using the internet as a research tool

◆ Communicating with experts via e-mail or letter writing

◆ Using information books

◆ Inviting a professional or expert into the classroom

◆ Visiting a place of expertise e.g. a castle

◆ Seeking information leaflets, posters or booklets

◆ Firsthand investigating using items or objects available

◆ Carrying out our own research

◆ Observing others or events

'How can we find out?' will be influenced and guided by the questions raised and the topic of learning.

What have we learned?

This question helps children to reflect on activities and experiences and identify new learning. It provides the perfect opportunity to evaluate activities and experiences. Did we find out the answer to how do we speak? What else did we find out? How did we find out? Did we learn a new skill? What was the most interesting thing you learned? Did anything surprise you?

Reflecting and evaluating enables the next step in the learning journey to be planned as children discuss what they have found out and if it leads to something else they would like to know. This cyclical approach continues as children find out more – it raises new questions and thoughts.

How could we share our learning? Handing this responsibility over to groups of children (particularly effective in Key Stage Two) supports a sense of ownership. Learners could decide to create a presentation, jingle, film, poster, information leaflet, etc. By equipping children with the skills to know how to use resources to best effect and linking all areas of learning together (as timings of film clips, design of leaflets or musical beats for a jingle) creates a real sense of meaning, purpose and ownership.

The KWFL method was popularised by David Wray and Maureen Lewis, and included in the training programme for the introduction of the Literacy Strategy:

'These grids have been shown to be useful tools in self assessment and involving children in their own learning.'
Assessment For Learning – Wigan Schoolsonline

The KWFL approach was commented on favourably by OfSTED in 2007 – the curriculum was judged as outstanding and the use of the KWFL approach to personalising learning was evident in the following statements:

'The school has created an innovative and exciting curriculum that matches pupils' needs and interests.' OfSTED 2007

'The way topics start with pupils' ideas about what they already know and what they would like to learn leads purposefully into the activities they will take part in to achieve their objective.'
OfSTED 2007

Where will questioning lead to in your setting?

The enthusiasm, satisfaction and greater understanding of individual children that can result from some of the approaches outlined in this book, are infectious. Each individual learner brings about a whole new and unknown path of shared discovery; practitioners and children learn and develop together, from and alongside one another.

I'll leave you with this: Evie, now 19 months, saw fireworks for the very first time and watched with amazement, occasionally shouting 'Bang! Bang!'. When they had finished she exclaimed 'Gone!' then using her experience of gone, she questioned 'Sleep?' 'Work?'

Bibliography

How Children Learn John Holt

Toxic Childhood Sue Palmer

Detoxing Childhood Sue Palmer

How do they walk on hat sand? Suffolk Advisory Service

Creativity across the primary curriculum Anna Craft

Teaching and Learning through Multiple Intelligences Linda Campbell, Bruce Campbell and Dee Dickinson

Early Childhood Education Tina Bruce

Smart Moves Why learning is not all in your head Carla Hannaford

The Thinking Child Resource Book Nicola Call with Sally Featherstone

The Brain's Behind It Alistair Smith

Exercising Muscles and Minds Marjorie Ouvry

Colour of my dreams by Peter Dixon

Learning without limits Susan Hart, Annabelle Dixon, Mary Jane Drummond & Donald McIntyre

The little book of Investigations Sally Featherstone

Early Years Educator – Volume 10 No 6

Great for finding out more...

Teaching Thinking and Creativity Magazine published by Imaginative Minds – informative articles sharing and discussing all aspects of creative teaching and learning.

Early Years Educator Magazine published monthly by MA Education – Informative, practical and real examples of effective learning within the EYFS.

50 Exciting ways to... by Helen Bromley. A fabulous range of books, rich with practical activities and ideas, to support exploration and inspiration.

Problem Solving by Margaret Martin – Great activities and example questions for developing problem solving and higher order thinking skills.

Glossary

Cognitive – construction of thought processes

Early Years Foundation Stage/EYFS – The welfare and learning and development structure, for children from 0-5 years, followed by early years providers and schools.

Key Stage One – Years One and Years Two (5-7 years) in maintained schools in England

Ownership – being and feeling like the owner (of direction and learning experiences)

Practitioner – an adult who works with children in a setting

Setting – Any out-of-home provider of education and care for children from birth to five, including playgroups, nursery, schools in the independent, private or voluntary sector and maintained schools in England.

Synthesis – linking ideas together